I0621254

Cultivating Confidence from the Lord

in Life, through Trials, as Entrepreneurs

Karen Lindwall-Bourg, PhD
Danika Deva

Written with members of
The National Association of Christian Women Entrepreneurs

Copyright 2023. Written by members of the National Association of Christian Women Entrepreneurs

All rights reserved. No part of this book may be reproduced or used in any manner without written permission of the copyright owner except for the use of quotations in a book review.

NOTICE OF LIABILITY

The information in this book is distributed on an "as is" basis, for informational purposes only, without warranty. While every precaution has been taken in the production of this book, neither the copyright owner nor the publisher shall have any liability to any person or entity with respect to any liability, loss, or damage caused or alleged to be caused directly or indirectly by the information contained in this book.

BIBLE PERMISSIONS

Scriptures marked AMP are taken from the AMPLIFIED BIBLE (AMP): Scripture taken from the AMPLIFIED® BIBLE, Copyright © 1954, 1958, 1962, 1964, 1965, 1987 by the Lockman Foundation Used by Permission. www.Lockman.org

Scriptures marked CEV are taken from the CONTEMPORARY ENGLISH VERSION (CEV): Scripture taken from the CONTEMPORARY ENGLISH VERSION copyright© 1995 by the American Bible Society. Used by permission.

Scriptures marked CJB are taken from the COMPLETE JEWISH BIBLE (CJB): Scripture taken from the COMPLETE JEWISH BIBLE, copyright© 1998 by David H. Stern. Published by Jewish New Testament Publications, Inc. www.messianicjewish.net/ jntp. Distributed by Messianic Jewish Resources Int'l. www.messianicjewish.net. All rights reserved. Used by permission.

Scriptures marked ESV are taken from the THE HOLY BIBLE, ENGLISH STANDARD VERSION (ESV): Scriptures taken from THE HOLY BIBLE, ENGLISH STANDARD VERSION ® Copyright© 2001 by Crossway, a publishing ministry of Good News Publishers. Used by permission.

Scriptures marked KJV are taken from the KING JAMES VERSION (KJV): KING JAMES VERSION, public domain.
Scriptures marked NAS are taken from the NEW AMERICAN STANDARD (NAS): Scripture taken from the NEW AMERICAN STANDARD BIBLE®, copyright© 1960, 1962, 1963, 1968, 1971, 1972, 1973, 1975, 1977, 1995 by The Lockman Foundation. Used by permission.

Scriptures marked NIV are taken from the NEW INTERNATIONAL VERSION (NIV): Scripture taken from THE HOLY BIBLE, NEW INTERNATIONAL VERSION ®. Copyright© 1973, 1978, 1984, 2011 by Biblica, Inc.™. Used by permission of Zondervan.

Scriptures marked NLT are taken from the HOLY BIBLE, NEW LIVING TRANSLATION (NLT): Scriptures taken from the HOLY BIBLE, NEW LIVING TRANSLATION, Copyright© 1996, 2004, 2007 by Tyndale House Foundation. Used by permission of Tyndale House Publishers, Inc., Carol Stream, Illinois 60188. All rights reserved. Used by permission.

Scripture quotations marked TPT are from The Passion Translation®. Copyright © 2017, 2018, 2020 by Passion & Fire Ministries, Inc. Used by permission. All rights reserved. ThePassionTranslation.com.

PUBLISHED BY

RHEMA Publishing House

www.rhemapublishinghouse.com

Cover design by Lisa Thomson;
Interior Design by Lee Desmond

ISBN: 979-8-9851550-0-6   paperback;
ISBN: 979-8-9851550-1-3   ebook

Dedication

God Bless Christian Women Entrepreneurs everywhere!

I couldn't have succeeded in entrepreneurship, especially in writing & publishing, without the women who supported me as our NACWE Team from 2017-2022.

Callie Revell
Christine Dupree
Courtenay Collins
Danika Deva
Eleina Shinn Rose
Jasmine Tosseth-Smith
Janie Owen-Bugh
Jessica Gallant
Jessica Hammock
Kathy Hadzibajric
Kathy Owen-Gifford
Lee Desmond
Lisa Thomson
Niki Banning
Valerie Riese

You have blessed me, I have grown—May God bless you right back!

The Lord bless you, and keep you;
The Lord make His face shine on you,
And be gracious to you;
The Lord lift up His countenance on you,
And give you peace.

Numbers 6:24-26 NASB

Contents

Preface

Confidence

We need confidence to live and work and serve.

We need faith to live and work and serve. Isn't *faith* a word that would fit companionably into almost every sentence we utter when speaking the word *confidence*?

I believe oftentimes, when we haven't accomplished what we've dreamed of in life, through trials, and as entrepreneurs, it may not be because we didn't have a vision and a dream, and it may not be because we didn't have the proper capabilities and skills. It might be because we lack *confidence* to move forward with those capabilities through those visions.

Community Builds Confidence

As we seek community and connection in our lives, workplaces, and places of service, our goals may be similar. We want an intimate connection and don't want to feel alone in life or work. We look for a safe and equipped place to learn and grow, a place that will offer us the encouragement and education to take us to the next level and help us serve God and His people more effectively. We need a site, as growing entrepreneurs, where we can share what God has called us to do with those who need our offers—services, programs, products, and more. And we desire to live and work with like-minded people who want to pay it forward to others and give of our abundance in ministry and missions.

The following confidence-inspiring pages are written by members of the National Association of Christian Women Entrepreneurs (NACWE). We are primarily an online group that meets in person as often as we can. We focus on Four Pillars as we seek a place to connect for:

- Community
- Education
- Networking
- Missions

When we, as Christian women entrepreneurs through NACWE, have joined together under all four pillars, we have also most commonly sought to gain confidence to move forward and fulfill our dreams.

Every year since the organization was established in 2010, the leaders have sought the Lord for the theme of the year and broken that God-given theme into sub-themes for each month. Most recently, as the NACWE Team and I worked together, we felt led to focus on *confidence* for 2022. And every single week, as new Christian entrepreneurs offer insight in how to cultivate confidence from the Lord to be who He has called us to be and to do what He has called us to do in life, through trials, and as entrepreneurs, we've been amazed at the testimonies of transformation from our members and visitors.

Our key verse for 2022:

For the Lord will be your confidence
and will keep your foot from being caught.
Proverbs 3:26 (NASB)

Collaboration Builds Confidence

I love collaborative book projects. I've written books in community, and some of them honestly have flowed out of me in a single weekend. On my own, one of them took two and a half painstaking years! Writing books as a group can be an immense blessing. Everyone pitches in, and the various perspectives shared take us to amazing new places. All parties benefit, and we know that in working and educating ourselves together, we learn faster and respond and adapt more efficiently. We do better together than by going it alone. We are better together!

I hope you'll join us as leaders and members of the National Association of Christian Women Entrepreneurs share the insights the Lord has given to cultivate confidence from Him so that we are truly a blessing to Him and to others as we live and work and serve—even through trials and suffering—and especially in our businesses and ministries.

You have blessed us. May God bless you right back!

Karen Lindwall-Bourg
NACWE President 2017–2022
NACWE Sister for Life
https://nacwe.com?fpr=karen-78

A Special Note About This Anthology

Book anthologies or compilations can be tremendous blessings for those writing, editing, and reading. I suppose the possibilities for the various types of collaborative books are as numerous as there are compilers of collaborative books. There really are no hard and fast rules.

Most of the collaborative works I have led or written within have been very structured. In the latest one, the owner gave everyone the same topic, the same format, and the same questions to answer about that topic—so as you can imagine in that book there will be at least a dozen different perspectives on the very same subject. Each chapter will look the same and flow similarly for the reader. Each chapter will be close to the exact same word count or size.

That's not the case with this particular work. As the president of the National Association of Christian Women Entrepreneurs for five years, I chose a theme of the year—and sometimes sub themes based on each quarter of the year or even each month of the year—then reached out to various experts and asked them to present an educational webinar or seminar on that sub theme. You can imagine the immense blessings hearing from Christian women entrepreneurs across the world for the 12 years since NACWE began, the wealth of information and blessing that has been bestowed upon us by all.

God led us to choose for the year 2022 the theme of *confidence*, **to be who God has called us to be and to do what He has called us to do.** We didn't choose a single sub theme. We reached out to over 50 women (I hope you'll eventually hear from them all), and let them choose their own topic as God led them. We did the same thing when we asked them to write in these compilations.

I am sharing this with you, dear reader, because I want you to know before you begin each chapter that they won't all be similar, in many ways not at all—not in subject, not in length, not in depth or height or breadth. I think our shortest chapter was the size of a blog and less than 1000 words. I am confident our longest chapter will be turned into a solo published work. It's very researched, quite detailed, and requires some deep thought and patient study from each reader.

I hope you enjoy your journey to confidence from the Lord from these special women as much as I did.

~Karen

Introduction:

Such Confidence We Have Through Christ Toward God

Such confidence we have through Christ toward God.
2 Corinthians 3:4 (NASB)

Our Confidence is in HIM

With conviction, I can confidently say *true* confidence comes from the Lord and from no other source.

Early in our year—as Christian women, as we sought the Lord on the topic of confidence in life, through trials, and as entrepreneurs—someone asked, "Isn't confidence the same as faith?" Without writing a scholarly treatise on the comparison of these two words throughout the scriptures, I think I can safely say that confidence in God encompasses faith and so much more.

I'll leave the faith and confidence dissertation to someone else for now. And I encourage you to dive deep into your own study. Peruse this book and other books in the Cultivating Confidence series and take advantage of the many offerings on the topic of confidence from members of the National Association of Christian Women Entrepreneurs (NACWE). https://nacwe.com and on Facebook https://www.facebook.com/groups/nacwe

For the Lord will be your confidence
and will keep your foot from being caught.

Proverbs 3:26 (NASB)

What is Confidence?

Merriam-Webster Dictionary definitions will surely encourage you.

Confidence... According to the World

Confidence is support, particularly in a legislative body. A vote of confidence holds more weight, especially when that vote is unanimous.

It is a communication made in secret. Information shared in confidence is only shared with another or with a select few. It encompasses reliance on another's discretion. None of us wants to betray confidence. You want to be trusted. And when you tell a story in strictest confidence, you rely on the other to be discreet. Hopefully, it's a reciprocal relationship.

Confidence is a relation of trust or intimacy. You take each other into your confidence. I take my friend into my confidence.

It is a firm belief in the integrity, ability, effectiveness, or genuineness of someone or something. You place deep confidence, credence, and stock in your wise counselors and coaches. You wouldn't ask them for wise advice if you were uncertain of their wisdom.

Confidence is a quality or state of being certain; it is a state of mind in which you are free from doubt. I am confident and assured and certain with conviction that God's Words will not return void. He tells me so! Disbelief will cause me to hesitate to follow Him.

It is a feeling or consciousness of one's powers or a reliance on one's circumstances. I have perfect confidence that God will use the words in this anthology to encourage you.

Confidence is having great faith in oneself or one's abilities. I hope you have self-confidence—even a lifelong confidence—that enables you to achieve remarkable things despite powerful obstacles.

Self-doubts hinder you from being who God has called you to be and doing what He has called you to do.

It is faith or belief that one will act in a right, proper, or effective way. NACWE sisters had confidence in me as their president for five years. I have confidence in Heather as our new NACWE president.

... According to the Lord

How do our dictionary definitions compare to God's use of the word *confidence* throughout the Old and New Testaments?

I have every confidence that God's definitions of confidence will greatly inspire and encourage you.

In the scriptures, you are discouraged from putting trust in man, and you are encouraged to put your trust in God alone. You desire to be trustworthy as followers of Christ and to find others in whom you can trust.

There are seven different original lexicon words in Hebrew in the Old Testament for the word confidence:[1]

0982 חָטַב batach

0986 וֹחָטְבִן bittachown

03690 הָלְסָכ kiclah

04009 חָטְבַמ mibtach

03689 לָסָכ kecel

0985 הָחְטַב bitchah

0983 חַטַב betac

From the Old Testament, we learn...

For the Lord will be your confidence
and will keep your foot from being caught.

Proverbs 3:26 (NASB)

You are to put your confidence in God.

In 2 Kings 18:19–22, King Hezekiah was credited with confidence and trust in the Lord God as he reigned over Judah and was victorious against the enemy's invasion. Even the King of Assyria noticed and remarked on this confidence.

Job trusted in, feared, and revered God and was a man of integrity. Job 4:6 (ESV) says, *Is not your fear of God your confidence, And the integrity of your ways your hope?* Job trusted in God alone, not in gold or wealth, or the sun or moon, or in his own heart or hand. In fact, he said that to trust in gold or wealth, or the sun or moon, or in his own heart or hand, was to deny God above (Job 31: 24–28). See also Psalm 65.

Psalm 118:8–9 tells us it is better to trust in the Lord than to place confidence in man or in princes.

It is our confidence that through the pages of this and other Cultivating Confidence anthologies, you will steadfastly place your confidence in God.

Confidence in God comes with reward.

Your foot will not be caught (Proverbs 3:26). *You will have refuge* (Proverbs 14:26). *You will be saved and strengthened* (Isaiah 30:15).

It is our prayer that through these readings, you will reap amazing rewards from the Lord for your confidence!

God caused men to put their confidence in His trustworthy leaders.

In Judges 9:26, the men of Shechem put their confidence in Gaal, the son of Ebed.

It is our hope that you will connect with others worthy of your confidence and trust, and that others will place utmost confidence in you.

There are seven different original lexicon words in Greek in the New Testament for the word confidence:[2]

3954 παρρησία parrhesia

4006 πεποίθησις pepoithesis

3982 πείθω peitho

2292 θαρρέω tharrheo

4183 πολύς polus

5026 ταύτῃ taute

5287 ὑπόστασις hupostasis

From the New Testament, we learn:

This is the confidence which we have before Him, that, if we ask anything according to His will, He hears us. And if we know that He hears us in whatever we ask, we know that we have the requests which we have asked from Him.

1 John 5:14–15 (NASB)

You will be empowered, comforted, and led by the Lord.

Consider Paul's teachings in his books inspired by the Holy Spirit:

Confidence in the Lord will empower you to preach and teach the Gospel unhindered and with openness. (Acts 28:25–31; 2 Corinthians 1:15–24; Philippians 1, 2 Thessalonians 3). Confidence in the Lord will affirm your love for God and for others and complete your joy and the joy of others whom you serve and exhort (2 Corinthians 2:2–3; 2 Thessalonians 3; 1 John 3). Your ministry will be commended (2 Corinthians 6). Like Paul, you will be meek and gentle and bold with confidence as you work for the Lord (2 Corinthians 10, especially 2 Corinthians 10:1–2). You will be confident that in weakness and in strength the Lord will use you to further His Kingdom (2 Corinthians 11).

Your heart will be comforted, your spirit will be refreshed, you will rejoice, and you will have confidence in those you serve (2 Corinthians 7, especially 2 Corinthians 7:16). You will receive grace and generosity from those you serve (2 Corinthians 8, especially 2 Corinthians 8:22).

My goodness! 2 Corinthians seems to be the **confidence** book of the Bible!

In confidence, you will be led by and walk in the Spirit with love, joy, peace, patience, kindness, goodness, faithfulness, gentleness, and self-control (Galatians 5). You will have a boldness for stewardship and confident access through faith in Him and will not lose heart (Ephesians 3). Your life goal will be to "worship in the Spirit of God and glory in Christ Jesus," to know Christ Jesus as Lord, and press onward (Philippians 3). You will realize and receive a great reward in confidence (Hebrews 10:35).

It is our confidence that through the pages of this and other Cultivating Confidence anthologies, you will trust in and serve the Lord with new found assurance.

It is our hope that through the pages of this and other Cultivating Confidence anthologies, you will love and minister to others as He did.

You will have assurance.

Consider John's teachings in his books inspired by the Holy Spirit:

In confidence, you will have assurance that whatever you ask of the Lord, you will receive (1 John 3:21). You will be confident of and convinced of eternal life (1 John 2:28).

We trust that through the pages of this and other Cultivating Confidence anthologies, you will grow in faith with a newfound certainty in who God is and in who He has created you to be and what He has called you to do to further His Kingdom in your life, through various trials, and as entrepreneurs in business and ministry.

In this Book 1 of our Cultivating Confidence Series you'll read about gaining confidence

- through the wisdom of Proverbs
- in your God-given calling
- with a vision aligned with His
- as you surrender to God's call
- to reframe your mindset
- in the midst of warfare
- with a confident crown
- in financial stewardship and ownership
- with newfound freedom
- in God's plan for prosperity through the seven dimensions of health
- reaping the rewards of confidence in God
  while navigating life transitions with confidence

Cultivating Confidence in LIFE

Under this banner, in future books in the series, we'll talk about cultivating confidence in life to know God; to ask, seek, and knock when we need Him; to hear Him, believe Him, and obey Him; to understand His love for us; to invite Him in and ask with anticipation instead of expectation; to ask others for help; to accept the Lord's assignment for us, to be who He called us to be and to do what He has called us to do; to align with His precepts; to assess our God-given calling or mandate and reaffirm that purpose frequently; to understand our identity in Christ; to build on our God-given strengths; to affirm everything through His word and His people; to live and work under grace; to rest in Him; to put on the whole armor of God to prepare; to act in faith, hope, love, and love for His people; to have an attitude of gratitude; to steward all He has entrusted to us; to make Him known; and to trust Him with the results of our life! Contact us if there is another area in which confidence is desired.

Now may the God of hope fill you with all joy and peace in believing, so that you will abound in hope by the power of the Holy Spirit.

Romans 15:13 (NASB)

Cultivating Confidence through TRIALS

Under this banner, we'll talk about needing confidence from the Lord through various trials such as through self-discovery and self-improvement; in understanding feelings, values, and worth; for peacekeeping and peacemaking; for forgiveness; through difficult life events that cause grief, bereavement, and loss such as the death of a loved one, job loss, physical illness, conflict, and conflict resolution; through mental health issues such as pride, fear and worry, desire, abuse, addictions and compulsion, anxiety and panic, anger, boundaries, depression, guilt and shame, habits and behaviors, narcissism, and stress; and understanding the will of God through transitions and decision making, like the transition through college and career or from corporate to entrepreneurship, marriage relationships and parenting, semi-retirement and retirement (or "re-firement"), and more. In what other challenges of life do you need confidence? Feel free to reach out to us.

Therefore let us draw near with confidence to the throne of grace, so that we may receive mercy and find grace to help in time of need.

Hebrews 4:16 (NASB)

Be strong and courageous, do not be afraid or tremble at them, for the Lord your God is the one who goes with you. He will not fail you or forsake you.

Deuteronomy 31:6 (NASB)

Cultivating Confidence as ENTREPRENEURS

Under this banner, we'll talk about growing in godly confidence in business and ministry, to build a connected community; to hear, believe, and respond to obey God in business and ministry; identity and enemies of identity; influence and impact; messaging, branding, and building; working God's way fundamentals; our assignment and unique calling; alignment with His precepts; kingdom marketing, sales, sales conversations, closing the sale, pricing with purpose, client engagement, confrontation, generosity, and collaboration without competition; unlearning things that don't align with working God's way; cooperating with the greatness of God; saying yes, saying no; and more. What else can you think of that will help you grow in confidence and serve the Lord?

Whatever you do, do your work heartily, as for the Lord rather than for men, knowing that from the Lord you will receive the reward of the inheritance. It is the Lord Christ whom you serve.
Colossians 3:23-24 (NASB)

We'd love to help you cultivate confidence from the Lord in life, through trials, and as entrepreneurs. We'd love to hear testimonies of God-confidence from you. And, if you've been called by God to share words of confidence with others, we'd love to feature you in one of our next books in our Cultivating Confidence series. Please reach out to Karen Lindwall-Bourg at karen@rhema3eservices.com.

Now, let us take this opportunity in the next chapters to encourage you to gain confidence from the Lord.

Endnotes

1, 2: https://strongsconcordance.org

Chapter 1

Proverbs 3:26 - The Lord is Your Confidence

Karen Lindwall-Bourg

*For the Lord will be your confidence
and will keep your foot from being caught.*

Proverbs 3:26 (NASB)

- Where do you find confidence from God in life, in general?
- How do you seek and increase confidence from the Lord as you suffer various trials?
- What are some ways you cultivate confidence from the Lord as a Christian entrepreneur wanting to work God's way?

Women of the National Association of Christian Women Entrepreneurs (NACWE) chose Proverbs 3:26 (NASB) as our key verse for the year: ***For the Lord will be your confidence and will keep your foot from being caught.*** And the blessings that have poured from these words are too numerous to count. Let's continue to seek confidence from the Lord together.

We are to Intentionally Seek Confidence from the Lord

Hebrews 10:35 says, *Therefore, do not throw away your confidence, which has a great reward* (NASB). Wow! If this confidence which comes from the Lord can be *thrown away*, you must exercise great caution. And you conversely now know that you are to hold, keep, and even preserve and protect the confidence He offers you.

Cultivating confidence from the Lord to be who He has called you to be and to do what He has called you to do isn't a passive process. It's a very **active and intentional and purposeful quest** to know Him and to understand how He sees you.

It involves fervently seeking Him and asking Him where your confidence comes from. You can ask Him for anything aligned with His Word. You can ask Him for confidence.

Then, it requires hearing Him, believing Him, and obeying Him once you receive His reward of confidence and His direction.

And while it may seem a contradiction, it requires resting in Him—even resting from seeking—lest seeking becomes an idol or primary focus and you miss the confidence God wants you to receive.

Praise God!

When you diligently seek Him, **He answers with Himself!**

As we've heard from different experts every week in our NACWE Community & Education webinars, we've presented the theme of the year and the key verse of the year and then introduced the unique topic of the current presenter of the week.

Every single time I or one of the team members introduced the webinar with that key verse, I have felt a tug at my heart from the Lord to dive deeper into it and ask what He means when He says He will be your confidence and when He says your foot will not be caught. Before you hear from our expert presenters throughout the rest of this book, let's search further and ask God these very questions.

The Lord Will Be Your Confidence

Remember that the Lord will be your confidence (Proverbs 3:26 NASB). Remind yourself daily. The Passion Translation tells us

He is our confidence *in times of crisis*. None of us are immune to crises.

Other translations emphasize:

The Lord is your confidence.	NASB, Passion, ASV, CEB, CEBA, CSB, DBY, ESV, GW, HNV, JUB, KJVA, LEB, NAS, NKJV, NRS, NRSA, OJB, RSV, RSVA, TMB, TMBA, WBT, WEB
He is your security.	(He keeps you safe) NLT GNT, GNTA, NCV, WYC, YLT
He is your hope.	BBE
You can rely on God.	(You can rely on ADONAI) CJB
You can trust in Him.	(The LORD is the One you will trust in.) NIRV
He will be right with you.	MSG
God will be at your side.	NIV, RHE
He will be over you.	(He is OVER all our ways.) LXX
and	
He will keep you safe.	GNT, GNTA, NCV, WYC, YLT

Using key words from the above Bible translations, ask God for His confidence today.

Let's look at the surrounding verses in The Passion Translation.

Wisdom, Our Hiding Place

21

My child, never drift off course from these two goals for your life:
to walk in wisdom and to discover discernment.

The word translated as "discernment" here can also mean
"discretion, counsel, meditation, and purpose."
Don't ever forget how they empower you.

22

For they strengthen you inside and out
and inspire you to do what's right;

Or "adorn your neck."
The neck is a picture of our will and conscience.
You will be energized and refreshed by the healing they bring.

23

They give you living hope to guide you,
and not one of life's tests will cause you to stumble.

24

You will sleep like a baby, safe and sound—
your rest will be sweet and secure.

25

You will not be subject to terror, for it will not terrify you.
Nor will the disrespectful be able to push you aside,

26

because God is your confidence in times of crisis,
keeping your heart at rest in every situation.

Or "keeping your foot from being caught."

Ask the Lord for His wisdom first and foremost. He will give you discernment, wise counsel, and purpose. He will help you align your will and conscience with His will. He will "keep your heart at rest in every situation" as you build your confidence from Him.

What a Relief!

What a relief to know you have a God who is your confidence, your hope, your security. You can rely on Him and trust in Him at all times. He will keep you safe; He will be over you, be right with you, and be at your side at all times.

And [the Lord] Will Keep Your Foot From Being Caught

We remind each other as NACWE sisters every week that the Lord will keep your foot from being caught.

In comparison, the Passion Translation tells you He will keep your heart at rest in every situation. I have been convicted so often over the past three years about not being at rest in the Lord. Other translations tell you the Lord will keep your foot from being taken, from being taken in the net, from being snared, from being caught in a trap, from falling into a trap, and from being captured. The LXX version says *He shall establish thy foot that thou be not moved.* Other translations tell you He will keep you safe and sound.

When you receive confidence from the Lord:

You will not be caught.	NASB, CJB, NLT (caught in a trap), ESV, GW, NAS, NIRV, NKJV, NRS, NRSA, RSV, RSVA, YLT
You will not be taken.	ASV, BBE (taken in the net), DBY, HNV, JUB, KJV, KJVA, RHE, WEB, WYC
You will not be snared.	CEB, CEBA, CSB, NIV, OJB TMB, TMBA
You will not be captured.	LEB
You will not fall into a trap.	GNT, GNTA (or be trapped), NCV
You will not be moved.	He will establish your foot that you be not moved. LXX

The Lord will keep you.	32 of the 38 versions of the Bible I looked at on BibleGateway.com include the word *keep*
The Lord will establish you.	LXX
He will keep your heart at rest in every situation.	Passion
and	
He will keep you safe and sound!	MSG

Using key words from the above translations, ask God to *keep* you today.

Confidence in the LORD Comes With Blessings and Rewards

Blessings to enjoy as the Lord is your confidence can be found throughout Proverbs 3:13–35.

If you trust and obey, your Father will direct your path into the blessings He has planned for you.

The first of these blessings is **the true wealth that comes from wisdom** (vv. 13–18).

Another blessing is **harmony with God's creation** (vv. 19–20).

A third blessing is **the Father's providential care** (vv. 21–26). Because God directs your path, He is able to protect your path. When you surrender yourself to God, every part of you belongs to Him and you will be protected by Him. He will help you keep

- your eyes from wandering (v. 21),
- your neck from turning your face away from God's path (v. 22; see also Luke 9:53),

- your feet walking on the right path (vv. 23, 26), and even
- your backbone safe while you're sleeping (v. 24).

If something frightening suddenly happens,

- you won't be afraid (v. 25; see also Psalm 112:7; 121:3–6), because the Lord is protecting you;
- you will sleep (vv. 24, 26).

Another blessing is **a positive relationship with others** you enjoy when you walk in the wisdom of God (vv. 27–35).

In one of our NACWE Confidence webinars, we talked about the familiar adage that God says in His Word 365 times, one time for every day of the year, *Do not fear!*

In essence, He is saying, *Have confidence!* 365 times, one time for every day of the year. I love that!

Remember our key verse:

> *For the Lord will be your confidence*
> *and will keep your foot from being caught.*

Proverbs 3:26 (NASB)

This whole section is sometimes called **Wisdom is Our Hiding Place** (TPT) or **Never Walk Away** (MSG) or **The Rewards of Wisdom** (NASB).

In the New American Standard Version, we read:

21
My son, let them [wisdom and discernment] not vanish from your sight;
Keep sound wisdom and discretion,
22
So they will be life to your soul
And adornment to your neck.
23
Then you will walk in your way securely
And your foot will not stumble.
24
When you lie down, you will not be afraid;
When you lie down, your sleep will be sweet.
25
Do not be afraid of sudden fear
Nor of the onslaught of the wicked when it comes;
26
For the Lord will be your confidence
And will keep your foot from being caught.

Be Confident!

- Where do you find confidence from God in life, in general? **From the Lord.** *For the Lord will be your confidence and will keep your foot from being caught* (Proverbs 3:26).

- How do you find confidence from the Lord as you suffer various trials? **Through HIS Power** *"My grace is sufficient for you, for power is perfected in weakness." Most gladly, therefore, I will rather boast about my weaknesses, so that the power of Christ may dwell in me* (2 Corinthians 12:9).

- What are some ways you cultivate confidence from the Lord as a Christian entrepreneur wanting to work God's way? **In HIM, endure and obey;** then receive His reward! *Therefore, do not throw away your confidence, which has a great reward. For you have need of endurance, so that when you have done the will of God, you may receive what was promised* (Hebrews 10:35-36).

- Can you think of a time in your life when God gave you confidence and abundance? Claim this verse:

*Now to Him who is able to do far more abundantly
beyond all that we ask or think, according to the
power that works within us, to Him be the glory
in the church and in Christ Jesus to
all generations forever and ever*

Ephesians 3:20-21 (NASB)

- Can you think of a time when under great duress and suffering, God offered you confidence beyond your understanding? Remember His promises.

*28
Do you not know? Have you not heard?
The Everlasting God, the Lord, the Creator of the ends of the earth
Does not become weary or tired.
His understanding is inscrutable.
29
He gives strength to the weary,
And to him who lacks might He increases power.
30
Though youths grow weary and tired,
And vigorous young men stumble badly,
31
Yet those who wait for the Lord
Will gain new strength;
They will mount up with wings like eagles,
They will run and not get tired,
They will walk and not become weary.*

Isaiah 40:28–31 (NASB)

- Can you think of a time as a Christian entrepreneur when God led you with confidence to unexpected success? Consider His words:

11

'For I know the plans that I have for you,' declares the Lord, 'plans for welfare and not for calamity to give you a future and a hope.'

12

Then you will call upon Me and come and pray to Me, and I will listen to you.

13

You will seek Me and find Me when you search for Me with all your heart.

14

'I will be found by you,' declares the Lord, 'and I will restore your fortunes and will gather you from all the nations and from all the places where I have driven you,' declares the Lord, 'and I will bring you back to the place from where I sent you into exile.'

Jeremiah 29:11–14 (NASB)

Be Confident in the Lord!

Chapter 2

Confidence at Your Fingertips: Inspiring Scriptures from our Authors

*For the Lord will be your confidence
and will keep your foot from being caught.*

Proverbs 3:26 (NASB)

Preface – Proverbs 3:26 (TPT)

*God is your confidence in times of crisis,
keeping your heart at rest in every situation.*

Introduction – 2 Corinthians 3:4 (NASB)

Such confidence we have through Christ toward God.

Chapter 1 – Proverbs 3:26 (NASB)
The Lord is Your Confidence

*For the Lord will be your confidence
and will keep your foot from being caught.*

Chapter 3 – Ephesians 4:1-3 (NASB)
**Cultivating Confidence
in Your God-Given Calling: Hear, Believe, and Obey**

*Therefore I, the prisoner of the Lord, implore you to walk in a manner
worthy of the calling with which you have been called, with all humility and*

gentleness, with patience, showing tolerance for one another in love, being diligent to preserve the unity of the Spirit in the bond of peace.

Chapter 4 – Romans 8:38, 39 (NASB)
Walking with Confidence

For I am convinced that neither death, nor life, nor angels, nor principalities, nor things present, nor things to come, nor powers, nor height, nor depth, nor any other created thing will be able to separate us from the love of God that is in Christ Jesus our Lord.

Chapter 5 – 1 Thessalonians 5:24 (AMP)
Confidence to Surrender to God's Call

Faithful and absolutely trustworthy is he who is calling you to himself for your salvation, and he will do it. He will fulfill his call by making you holy, guarding you, watching over you, and protecting you as his own.

Chapter 6 – Isaiah 26:3 (NLT)
Confidence Through Your Mindset:
Reframing Your Mindset in a New Season...Or Anytime

*You will keep in perfect peace all who trust in you,
all his thoughts are fixed on you!*

Chapter 7 – 2 Corinthians 10:4-5 (KJV)
Maintaining God-Confidence in Warfare:
The Power of Remembering

For the weapons of our warfare are not carnal, but mighty through God to the pulling down of strongholds; casting down imaginations, and every high thing that exalteth itself against the knowledge of God and bringing into captivity every thought to the obedience of Christ.

Chapter 8 – Jeremiah 29:11 (NLT)
Finding a Crown of Confidence ...Once Again

"For I know the plans I have for you," says the Lord.
"They are plans for good and not for disaster,
to give you a future and a hope."

Chapter 9 – Matthew 6:33 (KJV)
Confidence in Finances: Stewardship Versus Ownership

But seek ye first the kingdom of God,
and his righteousness;
And all these things shall be added unto you.

Chapter 10 – John 8:36 (NLT)
Confidence Through Freedom

So if the Son sets you free, you are truly free.

Chapters 11 & 12
Cultivating Confidence in God's
Plan for Your Prosperity: Experiencing True Prosperity
in the Seven Dimensions of Health

3 John 1:2 (CJB)

Dear friend, I am praying that everything prosper with you and
that you be in good health, as I know you are prospering spiritually.

Genesis 2:2, 3 (CJB)

On the seventh day God was finished with his work which he had made,
so he rested on the seventh day from all his work which he had made.
God blessed the seventh day and separated it as holy; because on that
day God rested from all his work which he had created,
so that it itself could produce [prosper].

Chapter 13 – Hebrews 10:35, 36 (NIV)
The Rewards of Confidence in God

So do not throw away your confidence; it will be richly rewarded. You need to persevere so that when you have done the will of God, you will receive what he has promised.

Chapter 14 – Isaiah 40:31 (NASB)
Navigating Life Transitions With Confidence

Yet those who wait for the Lord will gain new strength; they will mount up with wings like eagles, they will run and not get tired, they will walk and not become weary.

Chapter 3

Cultivating Confidence in Your God-Given Calling: Hear, Believe, and Obey

Karen Lindwall-Bourg

*Therefore I, the prisoner of the Lord, implore you to walk in a manner
worthy of the calling with which you have been called,
with all humility and gentleness, with patience,
showing tolerance for one another in love,
being diligent to preserve the unity of the Spirit
in the bond of peace.*

Ephesians 4:1-3 (NASB)

For the entire year of 2022 in our Christian women entrepreneur group, we focused on the theme *Cultivating Confidence in our God-given Calling* to be who He has called us to be and to do what He has called us to do. It turned out to be a life-changing experience for many of us. And it is a privilege to share the journey with you.

- In Life: Do you sometimes look at the big picture and freeze?
- Through Suffering: Do you sometimes struggle under the trials of life—small and big—and wonder where you will find the strength to continue on?
- As God's Servant: As a servant in business or ministry, have you started and stopped and started and stopped different projects and wondered why and how to get back on track?

Proverbs 3:26 in the NASB says, *For the Lord will be your confidence and will keep your foot from being caught.*

The entire chapter of Proverbs 3 is titled *The Rewards of Wisdom.* And the wisest man on earth, Solomon, gives advice to his sons and to us to seek wisdom first.

Only through the wisdom given to us as Christian entrepreneurs by the Lord can we cultivate the confidence needed to be who He has called us to be and to do what He has called us to do.

To hold the reins of confidence to reign in life, through trials, and as servants in business and ministry, we must hear, believe, and obey God as He leads.

Easier said than done. How do we cultivate confidence to assuredly hear, confidently believe, and diligently obey?

Cultivating Confidence in Life

Life can be so complicated, so busy, so involved!
but
Praise God! We can hear, believe, and obey with faith. He is our Source of confidence. He is THEE SOURCE of confidence.

In LIFE, the confident follower of God hears the Lord, believes His words, and responds to God in obedience—because surely our lives and our work and ministry must begin with who God is and who we are in Christ.

In 2 Corinthians 3:4 we read, *Such confidence we have through Christ toward God.* Paul goes on to state that our ability is from God. He actually uses the word *adequacy* in the NASB. I was at a women's conference where one of the leaders stated that God doesn't always ask us if we *can* do what He has called us to do; He most often asks us if we are *willing* to do what He has called us to do. Paul explains that we're not capable enough to do anything in our own strength, but our ability comes from God or *flows from God's empowering presence*. The Lord makes us able to do what He has called us to do.

Takes a bit of the pressure off, doesn't it?

God calls and equips us. Our responsibility is to hear, believe, and obey.

Consider:

Hear Him

He promises to answer. If we listen, He promises we will hear great things.

> *Call to me and I will answer you, and will tell you great and hidden things that you have not known.*
> Jeremiah 33:3 ESV

Hearing God requires us to purposefully and intentionally meet with Him as the CEE—Chief Executive of Everything—for our lives on a regular and very intimate basis. I don't know about you, but I have a tendency to sit down with the Lord and ask Him a question, and so often I see a vision of the Lord (as I have begun to run out the door toward the next shiny object) imploring me or reaching out to me as if to say, "Karen, you asked Me a question. I was getting ready to answer it, but you ran off before you heard My answer!"

I asked God some very specific questions as I felt Him prodding me to make some pretty significant changes in the National Association of Christian Women Entrepreneurs (NACWE) this year, and I heard His answers:

- **when** I was willing to sit still long enough, and
- **when** I was willing to acknowledge His answers, especially as some of them were not exactly what I wanted to hear.

What will it take for you to hear from the Lord in this season—perhaps more intimately than you've ever heard Him before?

Take a moment to talk to the Lord about this.

Believe Him

I love the scripture, *Immediately the boy's father cried out and said, "I do believe; help my unbelief"* (Mark 9:24). I have found myself praying that prayer more often in the last 18 months than ever before as the Lord has prompted me to make some very significant changes with this organization. Earlier, if you'd asked me if I heard what the Lord said, I would have to admit that yes, I had. If you'd asked me if I was walking in obedience in what the Lord said, I would have to admit that yes, I was. If you'd asked me if I believed what God was asking me to do and that He would carry me through it, I would've also given you a resounding *Yes*; but on closer inspection, I would've had to say no. Am I right? If I believed what I heard—truly believed it—I would have acted on it much sooner and with utmost confidence.

We don't get to read how the boy's father's unbelief was helped after Jesus healed his son, but I can only imagine his faith increased. The greater challenge will be when Jesus asks us to believe and does not perform a miracle immediately.

Are there areas in which you've heard from the Lord in preparation for this new season but unbelief has hindered you from moving forward? Take a moment to talk to the Lord about this.

Obey Him

At this very same women's retreat, I walked away with multiple blessings, but the primary blessing was a realization that I had not been fully obedient to the Lord and what He called me to do. Was I doing the work He had called me to, yes, I was. And I was, like a petulant child, kicking and screaming most of the way and then wondering why I wasn't fulfilled. As hard as it was to admit disobedience to the women at the retreat—and especially to the Lord—it gave me such freedom, purpose, and resolve to continue on the path God laid before me. Once I obeyed fully, the blessings poured forth. Yes, there is blessing in obedience!

Leviticus 26:3-4 (NASB) states, *If you walk in My statutes and keep My commandments so as to carry them out, then I shall give you rains in their season, so that the land will yield its produce and the trees of the field will bear their fruit.* What a blessing! Then verses 5-13 go on to list additional blessings that will follow obedience:

- Seasonal rains
- Produce and fruit
- Lasting harvest
- Food to eat "to the full"
- Secure living in your land
- Peace in your land
- Freedom from harmful beasts in the land
- No war in the land
- Victory in battle
- Fruitfulness and multiplication
- God's covenant confirmed with you
- Newness
- God will make His dwelling among you.
- His soul will not reject you.
- He will walk among you and be your God, and you shall be His people.
- He will bring you out of captivity and slavery.
- He will break the bars of your yoke and make you walk erect.

Amen to all of these blessings!

Will you ask the Lord in the next few moments to reveal to you an area of disobedience and offer Him your obedience?

Cultivating Confidence through Trials

Suffering can seem to hinder us from fulfilling our God-given calling.
and
Praise God! We can hear, believe and obey with hope.
His hand is intimately mixed up in our troubles.
And He answers with Himself.

Through TRIALS, the confident follower of God overcomes suffering and triumphs over deception and obstacles in daily life because the struggles of life are somewhat universal to us all, but also unique for every one of us.

In 2 Corinthians 4, we read of the confidence of Paul's ministry in spite of many trials. Lest we think his trials were mild, he describes them as affliction, perplexing, persecution, struck down, being delivered over to death. Because he believed in Jesus and His Words, he continued to be confident to minister, to speak, to die. He encourages us not to lose heart or hope when facing various sufferings of this world.

Therefore we do not lose heart, but though our outer man is decaying, yet our inner man is being renewed day by day. For momentary, light affliction is producing for us an eternal weight of glory far beyond all comparison, while we look not at the things which are seen, but at the things which are not seen; for the things which are seen are temporal, but the things which are not seen are eternal.

2 Corinthians 4:16-18 (NASB)

Consider:

God is our Firm Foundation when trials come.

We definitely learn from the book of Job that our lives are *short of days and full of trouble* (Job 14:1). But we also learn that God's hand is intimately mixed up in all our troubles. We are perplexed by troubles, wondering why things are happening and where God is and what He is doing. We wonder what faith looks like and how the Lord shows up during the tumultuous journeys that we travel.

And we are so grateful to know that God is our firm foundation when trials come!

God never promises that our lives will be safe, easy, peaceful, healthy, and prosperous. Therefore, we cannot read God's favor or disfavor by assessing how troubled a person's life is.

At the same time, it's obvious from scripture and experience that we also experience joys and good gifts from God's hand—family, friends, food, health, moments of beauty, great opportunities, love, laughter, work, rest. We enjoy all good gifts with gratitude in our hearts. Therefore, we cannot read God's favor or disfavor by assessing how easy and trouble-free a person's life is.

Thankfully, it's obvious from scripture and it can become deeply rooted in our experience that God speaks and acts through affliction. In his book *The Problem of Pain,* C.S. Lewis said, "... pain insists upon being attended to. God whispers to us in our pleasures, speaks in our conscience, but shouts in our pain: it is His megaphone to rouse a deaf world."[1] Therefore, we **can** read God's favor or disfavor by noticing how a person responds to affliction. Are there people in your life that are fine examples of this? (I immediately think of my husband Tim, my parents, and friends Danika and Michelle.)

God's Hand is intimately holding us up in our troubles. To survive, we must receive His nourishment every day. His answer may seem painfully slow. His answer has to be lived out over time and uniquely by each of us. His answer involves changing us into a different kind of person. He imparts His answer upon our hearts.

In his book *God's Grace in Your Suffering*, Dave Powlison said:

> ... I guarantee this: God will surprise you. He will make you stop. You will struggle. He will bring you up short. You will hurt. He will take His time. You will grow in insight and in love. He will deeply delight you. You will find the process harder than you ever imagined and better. Goodness and mercy will follow you all the days of your life. At the end of the long road you will come home at last. No matter how many times you've heard it, no matter how long you've known, no matter how well you can say it, God's answer will come to mean something better than you could ever imagine.[because] He answers with Himself.[2]

Remembering God's promises and provisions increases our confidence.

To find confidence from the Lord, especially during times of intense suffering, we *remember God's promises and provisions.*

Consider Asaph's responses to trials in Psalm 77:

- Asaph suffered and was overwhelmed. He sought the Lord. You, too, can diligently search for God even when times are terrible and the effort seems worthless. Seek Him even when you don't feel like it.

- Asaph lacked confidence in God, so he invited Him in. He said, "I keep looking for you, God, but your comforting grace is nowhere to be found!" I absolutely love how God gives you words to utter throughout the Psalms, especially when you feel speechless. You also are allowed to utter desperate concerns and invitations to your loving God. He wants to hear from you.

- Asaph regained confidence by remembering God. He began to list remembrances of God's holiness, of His miraculous works, of times He redeemed and rescued him, and of times He led and continued to lead him by His loving hand and through others. You can find renewed confidence by remembering God's holiness, wonderful works, redemption, rescue, and loving hand.

In your struggles last year, and in your trials to come this year, how can you remember the Lord to regain confidence as He answers with Himself?

Take a moment to talk to the Lord about this.

What is the best way to walk the journey—for yourself and others?

Cultivating Confidence as Entrepreneurs

As a Christian ENTREPRENEUR, the confident follower of God excels in entrepreneurship or business and ministry with a Kingdom Heart, because working God's way is the only way—we know because we've tried it our way for way too long!

Entrepreneurship and our work in business and ministry can be a constant challenge. Praise God that we can Hear, Believe and Obey with love. In 1 Peter 4:1-11 (NASB, 1995) we read,

Keep Fervent in Your Love

Therefore, since Christ has suffered in the flesh, arm yourselves also with the same purpose, because he who has suffered in the flesh has ceased from sin, so as to live the rest of the time in the flesh no longer for the lusts of men, but for the will of God…The end of all things is near; therefore, be of sound judgment and sober spirit for the purpose of prayer. Above all, keep fervent in your love for one another, because love covers a multitude of sins. Be hospitable to one another without complaint. As each one has received a special gift, employ it in serving one another as good stewards of the manifold grace of God. Whoever speaks, is to do so as one who is speaking the utterances of God; whoever serves is to do so as one who is serving by the strength which God supplies; so that in all things God may be glorified through Jesus Christ, to whom belongs the glory and dominion forever and ever. Amen.

In all we do, especially in the work we have been called to, we are to keep fervent in our love for God to glorify Him through Jesus Christ.

In all we do, especially in the work we have been called to, we are to love others fervently.

Serve the Lord; Serve His People

As Christian entrepreneurs, within your business, you serve God and minister to others. I've always considered my business to be my ministry.

Your ministry has to be managed like a business or it won't last very long. First of all, it's required by the city, county, state, country, and even international organizations that we live in and work through that we run our ministries in certain ways—keeping records, following the letter of the law, making reports, etc.

So, whether you consider your business a ministry or you believe your ministry is a business, you must conduct business in your organization in businesslike manners.

We work and minister *as for the Lord*.

Consider:

> *Whatever you do, do your work heartily,*
> *as for the Lord rather than for men.*

Colossians 3:23 (NASB)

In The Passion Translation it is written this way: *Put your heart and soul into every activity you do, as though you are doing it for the Lord himself and not merely for others.*

This verse commands us to work *as for the Lord*, and Paul doesn't make a distinction between whether you feel like your work is business or ministry. *As for the Lord* surely includes working and ministering according to the Lord's precepts and according to the laws of governing bodies, which we believe the Lord put into place—oftentimes whether we like them or not.

Ask God to Bless Your Work and Ministry.

Consider Jabez:

Jabez asked God to bless and enlarge his border, and God granted what he asked!

> *Jabez was more honorable than his brothers; and his mother called his name Jabez, saying, "Because I bore him in pain." Jabez called upon the God of Israel, saying, "Oh that You would bless me and enlarge my border, and that Your hand might be with me, and that You would keep me from harm so that it might not bring me pain!"*
> *And God granted what he asked.*

1 Chronicles 4:9-10

Don't you want your borders expanded? Personal, business, and ministry borders— personally, relationally, physically, professionally, financially, emotionally—Yes!

Do you believe if you ask, God will expand your borders? Hmmm… Maybe not so much?

It's Ultimately About Stewardship, Isn't It?

God promises our "**Return on Obedience (ROO)** is greater than our *Return on Investment (ROI).*"[3]

Stewardship is about service. *As each has received a gift, use it to serve one another, as good stewards of God's varied grace* (1 Peter 4:10 ESV).

Stewardship is your calling. *And God blessed them. And God said to them, "Be fruitful and multiply and fill the earth and subdue it and have dominion over the fish of the sea and over the birds of the heavens and over every living thing that moves on the earth"* Genesis 1:28 (ESV); And *The Lord God took the man and put him in the garden of Eden to work it and keep it* (Genesis 2:15 ESV).

Stewardship is rewarding. *The point is this: whoever sows sparingly will also reap sparingly, and whoever sows bountifully will also reap bountifully. Each one must give as he has decided in his heart, not reluctantly or under compulsion, for God loves a cheerful giver* (2 Corinthians 9:6-7 ESV).

Stewardship requires you to be obedient and well-informed, even educated.

Recall:

The Parable of the Talents

> *For it [entry into the Kingdom of Heaven v1-13] will be like a man going on a journey, who called his servants and entrusted to them his property. To one he gave five talents, to another two, to another one, to each according to his ability. Then he went away. He who had received the five talents went at once and traded with them, and he made five talents more. So also he who had the two talents made two talents more. But he who had received the one talent went and dug in the ground and hid his master's money.*

Matthew 25:14-30 (ESV)

He praised the servant with 10 talents and the servant with four talents. He chastised the servant who buried his talent. (No pun intended!) We are to steward what God gives us in ways that honor Him and bring Him glory, in ways that draw other people to Him, as we work and minister *as for the Lord* (again, from Colossians 3:23). Proper stewardship in obedience to God includes a promise.

You can't outgive God!

What we are given by God doesn't belong to us. And yet, He only asks of us a portion in return. To obediently tithe—another financial term that makes us sometimes cringe—whether we are tithing of our time and our resources and our income,

- requires that we have time, resources, and income—which in turn
- requires that we manage our businesses and ministries well—which in turn
- requires that we are good stewards of what God gives us—which in turn
- requires that we meet with God regularly asking Him for guidance: **HBO**—Hearing, Believing and Obeying Him**.**

Consider what God has to say about giving in Malachi 3:8-12.

You Have Robbed God

"Will a man rob God? Yet you are robbing Me! But you say, 'How have we robbed You?' In tithes and offerings. You are cursed with a curse, for you are robbing Me, the whole nation of you! Bring the whole tithe into the storehouse, so that there may be food in My house, and test Me now in this," says the Lord of hosts, "if I will not open for you the windows of heaven and pour out for you a blessing until it overflows. Then I will rebuke the devourer for you, so that it will not destroy the fruits of the ground; nor will your vine in the field cast its grapes," says the Lord of hosts. "All the nations will call you blessed, for you shall be a delightful land," says the Lord of hosts.

Malachi 3:8-12 (NASB)

God considers our offerings His own from the beginning, and He instituted the rule of the tithe to bless us.

Check out the great promise God gives to those who are faithful to give—He says that He will open the floodgates of heaven, and *pour out so much blessing that there will not be room enough to store it* (Malachi 3:10 ESV). The last time God threw open the floodgates of Heaven, it rained for 40 days and 40 nights—so when He says that He's going to bless us, we know that He means business.

It may be hard to see how God is going to bless us for our faithfulness in giving, but He is waiting for us to take a step of faith and believe that He makes good on His promises. In fact, this is one time in scripture where God gives us explicit permission to test Him: *…test Me now in this," says the Lord of hosts, "if I will not open for you the windows of heaven and pour out for you a blessing until it overflows"* (Malachi 3:10).

The miracle of giving is that when we give to God, He gives us abundantly more in return.

Is there an example in your business and ministry of this very precept and miracle?

My life example would be my mom, who was single and often seemed to barely make it month to month. We offered to help—and in her later years we did help—but I can't tell you how often she would say something like, "Last month, I needed $67 to make ends meet, and then in the mail, I received a note from someone, and guess what? It held $67!"

My business and ministry example would be our counseling practice. After running well with seven counselors, interns, and associates for 12 years, I felt the Lord calling me to become president of NACWE and to really give them my whole heart and attention for a period of time. I didn't need to be torn in both directions. So, in a matter of a month or two in 2019, I shut down about 90% of the practice. Those next few years were beyond blessed, beyond precious, and priceless!

Then in 2021, almost two years later, I felt God leading me to open the practice again, and it didn't take long before my client load was right where I wanted it to be. In obedience, I moved forward—with some specific questions for the Lord, as you can imagine. And, again, when I finally sat still long enough to hear Him, He answered. He's given me a new direction, and He used a couple of the women in NACWE to help me transition through and toward this new direction.

Remember to **HBO** - *Hear, Believe and Obey Him.*

Remember, your ROO (Return on Obedience) is greater than your ROI (Return on Investment).

Consider 2 Corinthians 9:1-11 again. Paul writes

> *The one who sows sparingly also reaps sparingly.*
> *But the one who sows bountifully, will also reap bountifully.*

God is able to provide you with every blessing in abundance, so that you may share abundantly in every good work. God gives us so much already, true, but He is also ready to give you so much more if you are willing to trust Him and plant that first seed…to give others some of what God has given you.

> *He is no fool who gives what he cannot keep to gain*
> *that which he cannot lose.*[4]

Jim Elliot

Endnotes

1. C.S. Lewis, The Problem of Pain, Kindle edition

2. David Powlison, God's Grace in Your Suffering, Crossway. Kindle edition.

3. Tasha Glover, Brand with Grace, https://tashaglover.com

4. Jim Elliot, The Journals of Jim Elliot, Baker Publishing Group, Kindle edition

Chapter 4

Walking With Confidence

Lee Desmond

For I am convinced that neither death, nor life, nor angels, nor principalities, nor things present, nor things to come, nor powers, nor height, nor depth, nor any other created thing will be able to separate us from the love of God that is in Christ Jesus our Lord.

Romans 8:38-39 (NASB)

"God isn't often in the business of taking [pain] away. Instead, he adds to it. He is more of a giver than a taker. He doesn't take away my darkness, he adds light. He doesn't spare me of thirst, he brings water. He doesn't cure my loneliness, he comes near."– Jane Marczewski *

- Is what you are called to and gifted with leading you closer to the Lord?
- Do you know that you know that you know God's unfailing love for you above all else?
- Are you taking time to sit quietly at the feet of Jesus?

Clear, Convinced, and Confident

I started wearing reading glasses when I turned 40. Almost overnight, my eyes changed, and written words looked fuzzy and unclear. I didn't want to admit that my vision was getting weaker, but life became limited pretty quickly, so the glasses went on. Without them, I lost confidence to perform everyday tasks well—reading a recipe, writing a check, driving anywhere. I needed to make a change for life to become clear again. I didn't realize, until I got my glasses, just how much help I needed, and glasses were a gift that gave my sight back. And when I remember where I put them, they help me see important parts of my life, and for that I am grateful.

Just like my vision of the world changed almost overnight, the Lord often reminds me that I need to redirect, re-*view* my life. I still need clarity in so many areas, and sight is only one of them. It's easy to become blinded or short-sighted when I make others or service my priority—friends, relationships, church, committees, work. These are often life-giving and meaningful, purposeful, safe. They define us and give us focus, and those are good things. But if we become so entrenched in these good things, our busyness takes us away from the whole reason we're busy—Jesus. If we don't step back for a different view, we can become almost crippled, we lose confidence in the next steps. And what happens? We easily fall.

When I read Romans 8:28, the word "convinced" pops out at me. I think "confident" could be easily substituted here: *For I am **confident** that nothing can separate us from the love of God.*

Return...and Rest

As someone who is still working out my salvation and learning to walk in Redemption, listening for God's still, small voice requires that I protect that stillness, that quiet.

Be still (cease striving) and know that I am God.

Psalm 46:10a (ESV, NASB)

When the busyness of life puts us in a place of burden, God desires to restore us to Himself; *"He adds light... He brings water... He comes near."* If all the activity of life keeps us from seeing that it's time to *rest* and *trust,* then what we do is as a loud noise, and we can easily lose sight of the God who made us and loves us beyond measure. As we are still before Him—in that quiet place where He is waiting—He will restore our hearts and minds with the assurance that He is continually refining us into the people He has created us to be, doing the work He has called us to. *In returning and rest you shall be saved; in quietness and trust shall be your strength* (Isaiah 30:15, ESV). Quietness, rest, and trust **saves** us.

An old Collegiate Dictionary defined *confidence*, paraphrased, as "living in a state of trust." Dictionary.com says this: Confidence:... *confidence* comes from Latin, specifically the noun *confidential from* the verb *confidere* "**to confide**." ... the verb *fidere* means "**to trust**." To **confide** and to **trust**—what we do when we sit at Jesus' feet, when we are still before Him and put all of the distractions of our lives behind us for a little while. As someone who is still working out my salvation and learning to walk in Redemption, listening for God's still, small voice requires that I protect that stillness, that quiet—to **confide** in Him and **trust** His work in my life—so my heart and mind will gain confidence that He is always speaking to my soul.

I think I'm beginning to see more clearly, and I even see some things that were never clear before. My glasses may not always be where I need them, but I'm sure glad I have them. And I'm thankful to God for His vision—because His perspective is what gives me the confidence to walk the path He created.

Endnote

* Jane Marczewski, from her blog post "Bald Girl in the Dark" October 30, 2020
nightbirde.com

Lee Desmond is the Managing Director and Editor of RHEMA Publishing House. She loves words, especially when they're encouraging and used well. She loves anything DIY, flower gardening, and feeding people around her table. She's been married for 37 years to Chuck, has five wonderful adult kids and seven beautiful grands (so far). When she isn't enjoying her lake view with her cup of coffee & chicory, you'll find her working on a new home project or face-timing with her grandchildren.

https://lee-desmond/blog

Chapter 5

Confidence to Surrender
to God's Call

Heather Rosson

*Faithful and absolutely trustworthy is He who is calling you to Himself
for your salvation, and He will do it. He will fulfill His call
by making you holy, guarding you, watching over you,
and protecting you as His own.*

1 Thessalonians 5:24 (AMP)

- Have you ever known that you were not equipped to do what God was calling you to do… yet?
- Has your first reaction ever been "Who me?" when God has called you to do something?
- Did you say *yes* to Jesus even when afraid?

I don't know about you, but every time I talk to someone who has experienced a call from God in their lives, I learn that they started out with a little bit of hesitation, a little bit of trepidation. It's not that they questioned God's call, but that the call seemed so big or so foreign that they just didn't know what to do with it.

My pastor tells the story of when he was called to come to Tucson, Arizona from Michigan. He met with the board at the church in Tucson to interview for candidacy as the new lead pastor. He then went back to his hotel room that night and sobbed: "Not here, God, please not here."

The reality is that he knew well enough that God was calling him to Tucson; but it wasn't in my pastor's own vision; it wasn't in his plans for his life. Fifteen years later, he would tell you that there's no place he'd rather be than Tucson. He loves this community. God always has that bigger vision for us, and a bigger plan. Yet how often we instead run a different narrative in our heads, the one that starts, "Oh no, I can't do that!"

When We Surrender

We know that God causes everything to work together for the good of those who love God and are called according to his purpose for them.

Romans 8:28 (NLT)

We can stand confident in God's call when we surrender our will to His will. We should know by now that surrender always works out for the best. When we surrender, "*We know that God causes everything to work together for the good of those who love God and are called according to his purpose for them*" (Romans 8:28, NLT). And the beautiful reality is that if we are following what God wants us to do, He will give us the desires of our heart as well as a community around us to support our ability to make that impact happen.

Still, He often has to push to get us to the place of surrender—to see what He has in mind and allow us to accept it when the time is right. This is what happened to me when God called me to be the president of the National Association of Christian Women Entrepreneurs (NACWE). Karen, the second president of NACWE and author of this book, first started talking to me in the summer of 2021 about wanting to move on from NACWE and looking for someone to take it over. At that time, I thought, "Hmmm, that might be me." I decided (that's right, *I* decided) that this might be something I'd like to explore. But when I called Karen—even before I could say a word about my potential interest—she said: "I think I found some-one to head up NACWE!" She told me who it was, and I congratulated her, thinking both that God had shut the door and maybe I had dodged a bullet.

The reality is that God didn't shut the door, he just knew it wasn't time yet. God knew Karen wasn't ready . . . I wasn't ready. It turned out that the person she had found to take over the organization had withdrawn and Karen would continue to lead the group for a while. And the reality was also that I had a few more things I needed to learn. Had we done this on my timeframe, according to *my* wishes, I wouldn't have had the God-given vision for NACWE that I have now.

So I went all-in to something else, building my own marketing agency—*Becoming Irresistible*. I became (and still am) a success-ful marketing strategist. I coach clients on business and marketing strategy so that they can take their dream, create programs, and market their business in a way that both *sells* and is in alignment with who they are and their voice. My company was looking awe-some. I had just gotten all my branding done; I was moving forward; clients were calling me. Well, we know that just when we're smack dab in the middle of our comfort zone, God is getting ready to shake things up a little bit. That was the spring of 2022.

In March, Karen started talking with me again about how she was yearning to move on to other projects and needed someone to lead NACWE. She wasn't asking, or even hinting—she was just opening a window. But I said to her, "You know Karen I really wish I wanted to do this. I just don't." (Does this sound anything like my pastor?) I didn't want to shake things up, because I was sitting in the middle of my comfort zone. I had clients coming in, things were going well, my website looked great, and I was making money doing something I love. It's just that God had a different plan for me, and NACWE was going to be part of it.

A few weeks later, God woke me up at 3:33 a.m. and said, "Heather, it's you." I was like, "What do you mean God? It's not me. But again He said, "Heather, it's you."

And in this moment of *"Are you sure?"*—in that hesitation moment, that trepidation moment that had me out of bed pacing my house with nervous energy and praying—I asked, *"Why, God?"*

Everything was going so well. All I could think about was all those things we say to ourselves when God comes in and shakes up our plans. I didn't want to hear it.

Once it became a reasonable hour of the morning to do so, I reached out to Karen—because I knew if I didn't text her then, I wasn't going to do it at all. And we started a dialogue. I didn't share with her that God had told me it was in His plan, I just asked her to talk. The whole time I knew I had this calling compelling me, but I still wasn't owning it; I was hesitating.

But God allows us the time to absorb new things and to surrender our will, and He also works within our relationships to encourage us. Karen was invigorated by my interest; she saw so much potential in me. The next thing I knew, God began to download all these ideas into my brain, and I could be confident in His call because I knew I was not doing this on my own. The whole point of the conversation suddenly became clear: I was going to be able to facilitate an amazing network of community support for all of us.

Community

---

*You can be confident in His call because you know
that you are not doing this on your own.*

I felt the value of community almost as a visceral punch that day as ideas began to pour in to me. I should have known that Karen's interest, this community's interest, would buoy me, because God would never ask us to do any of this alone. He created us to be in relationships.

And at that moment I had my first idea for how to begin to lead NACWE. It was all about cake. I do love cake—especially chocolate. I get a small piece on my fork, close my eyes, put it in my mouth and slowly remove the fork. The chocolate pours over my tongue. It's creamy and decadent. There is nothing sweeter in that moment. But, a great cake takes many individual ingredients: flour, sugar, butter, chocolate, eggs, etc. Any one of these on its own is raw material, not cake. No one wants to eat a handful of flour, a stick of butter, or a cup of sugar. God works through the combination of ingredients and when we put these elements together, we get this gorgeous, delicious confection!

It hit me that day that each of us alone is like flour or butter or sugar. It takes all of us together to create a beautiful picture. We all will struggle from time to time with our calling. And we all need reminding to surrender to God in order to accomplish the goals we have for ourselves and for our businesses.

In the days since taking on this commitment, I have learned—by talking with members of our community—that being a Christian woman entrepreneur can be an extremely lonely place to function. At those times when it feels like you don't have anyone in your corner, it is sustaining to find God flowing through not just you, but through your connection with other people. For me, not just being a part of—but leading—this community of like-minded women working towards the same goals and dreams and holding the same values and priorities, has been profoundly satisfying and deeply affirming of my commitment to heed God's call. This is reinforced every time I connect with our members. When we connect for Wisdom Well Wednesdays, I am deeply moved by the thoughtful answers and the open sharing of ideas. When we connect for prayer, I am in awe of the ways in which God moves. When we connect to hear from a guest speaker, the wisdom that is shared is mind-blowing.

Impact

We know that our God-given purpose is to impact the world for good.

In living with this call, I have learned that the things this group needs to serve in their businesses are the same things its members need to serve God. In short, service to God is self-reinforcing. Accepting God's call to make a difference in the world through our businesses is not the kind of decision we make one day and then put in our back pocket; it's a continual recommitment. Implementing God's plan is tantamount to achieving your own fuller life. And it also results in better businesses.

For instance, God works through you to help you find a community. That community can help you feel supported and assist you with tools that help your business succeed. That successful business serves His will, because serving your community and your customer, is serving God's will. We know this, intuitively. We don't do business for the sake of doing business. In our NACWE meetings, whenever any member speaks, she talks of making an impact in the world. We know that our God-given purpose is to impact the world for good. No matter what your business model is, as a Christian entrepreneur we engage in service to humanity.

Income

In addition, because God desires us to impact the world, He equips us with what we need. A key piece of this is our revenue. Even if your business is highly ministry based, you still have a revenue motive. Don't think of revenue as standing in the way of your service and values; *it is a tool by which you achieve those values.* With God all things are possible. He works through our hands and feet. Think of it this way: businesses that aren't making money cannot keep going. It may sometimes feel uncomfortable to affirm your revenue goals, but, if you're not bringing in revenue to sustain your business (a business that supports you and your team who are dependent upon it), then your business is going to fall flat. You cannot have an impact on the world—the impact that God desires for you—if you can't stay open.

Education

Successful engagement as a businesswoman can allow for great confidence in our calling; and a key component of finding that confidence is our own education. I know that we're all really good at what we do. We are multi-talented: tech geeks, great writers, organizers, communicators, and coaches. But we still need the right kind of training, training that's specifically designed for us as Christian women. Just because we do what we do exceptionally well, doesn't mean none of us need to learn anything new. There are nuances to finding the right faith-based path when dealing with a world that is not always driven by principle. In my marketing world, for instance, I can testify that there are reputable practices and ones that are, well, less scrupulous. The way we learn and apply knowledge in each of our different crafts and skill sets can be different from the world at large because our priorities are often different.

We need the right kind of training—training that's specifically designed for us as Christian women.

The good news is that we are always in a state of learning, so we can always get what we need when it comes to education. NACWE takes the education of members seriously, so seriously in fact that we provide excellent education every single week. There is an entire vault of education available to our members. We have even had one member say that she built her entire business out of the NACWE classroom.

So we need the right kind of education that respects our values. We need to have the skills to serve our clients and community well. In the same way that the best cake is made in love, and with the highest quality ingredients, all the integrity and honesty that we can put into our business will serve us and God. These pillars work together, and the ways in which God works through you and your business, as well as the way your business and you work to support God's wishes, is self-reinforcing.

It's not that confidence in your calling allows you to succeed in business, but that business is the tool by which you reinforce your commitment to your calling.

You deserve a business that aligns with your values and beliefs.

Heather is the founder of Becoming Irresistible, a coaching and strategy business that guides impact-driven coaches in building powerful marketing strategies using proven systems and processes. She is also the President and CEO, Chief Experience Officer, of the National Association of Christian Women Entrepreneurs. https://nacwe.org

As a certified Lifeforming Leadership Coach and a Certified Master Marketer, Heather has empowered hundreds of entrepreneurs to connect their passion with God's purpose and create the life and business of their dreams. She believes we all have a message to share. That's why she helps her clients embrace marketing strategies that feel good (and actually work!).

Heather lives in Tucson, AZ with her husband and is the mother of three adult children (*Yay, they made it!*). She continues to serve her local church weekly and is active in her community. She is forever grateful for the opportunities God has given her. It is her prayer that she can continue to help others experience the same joy of knowing who they are and fulfilling their divine purpose.

https://heatherrosson.com

Confidence Through Your Mindset: Reframing Your Mindset in a New Season… or Anytime

Danika Deva

*You will keep in perfect peace all who trust in you,
all whose thoughts are fixed on you.*

Isaiah 26:3 (NLT)

- Does your mindset need a shift?
- Do you know how to reframe your mindset?
- Do you need help propelling yourself forward in life and business with a reframed mindset?

As you may notice, this chapter is uniquely written from the combined thoughts and experiences of members in the National Association of Christian Women Entrepreneurs webinar on mindset. It came out of questions posed and discussed about shifting our own mindset: first, by focusing on God, and then by intentionally looking at our own thoughts and patterns that need to shift so we can be confident women for the Kingdom.

This is me! What do you see? Well, not much because the picture is framed wrong. As you can see, this one needs to be reframed.

Reframe Your Mindset with Confidence

So it is with our hearts and minds. We can't move forward in life or business without the proper frame around us.

It doesn't start with chanting a mantra. It doesn't start with an up-sell. It doesn't start with empowering ourselves. It starts with HEART. Then it flows to our minds, actions, and words—and creates confidence.

We All Get Stuck

We all get stuck in our mindset at times. It can be because we are busy, out of focus, impatient, insecure, and more.

You see, once we get our hearts refocused, we can move ahead with everything else in our lives.

And ladies, the benefits are amazing

- Peace is a huge benefit. Peace in circumstances, our relationships, our homes, and our businesses (Isaiah 26:3).
- Clarity is another benefit, and who doesn't want that? When we align our hearts with the Father, clarity shows up.

- Some of the other benefits that the ladies in the NACWE webinar *Reframing our Mindset in the New Year…or Anytime* (January 11, 2022) mentioned were energy, momentum, the ability to see our circumstances externally instead of internally, and the ability to recognize lies and traps of the enemy. Whoa, what a list!

Why Do We Resist?

So if framing our mindset is so beneficial, why do we resist doing it, or not even think about it? Well, there are lots of reasons.

Sometimes it is our own internal conversation of *I don't feel enough*, or *I can't do this on my own.* It can also be unconscious. We may not even know we need to reframe our thinking. We think we see the pic as it is supposed to be (like the picture above).

Oftentimes, we are in process and learning to go within to see why, or we are working on it—but we are still not framing things correctly.

We resist change because resources are not available, because we are unfocused, distracted, fearful—or just plain confused about what to do.

And yes, sometimes we are just listening to the enemy! Are you with me?

So what practical steps can we take to shift our mindset and propel ourselves forward?

Practical Steps to Move Forward

Setting a routine can help shift your mindset, since a routine keeps you moving forward. Along with this, letting your brain in on the plan ahead of time helps, too. For example, saying to yourself, "It's okay that I feel uncomfortable right now."

We can take every thought captive by focusing on Christ. Asking ourselves, "What is the truth in this situation?" is a great start. Using this filter helps reframe the negative thoughts that run through our heads.

2 Corinthians 10:5 (NIV) states, *We demolish arguments and every pretension that sets itself up against the knowledge of God, and we take captive every thought to make it obedient to Christ.* We must focus on *taking every thought captive* so we don't get stuck.

What are some more verses from scripture that tell us to reframe our heartset and mindset?

> *And now, dear brothers and sisters, one final thing. Fix your thoughts on what is true, and honorable, and right, and pure, and lovely, and admirable. Think about things that are excellent and worthy of praise.*

Philippians 4:8 (NLT)

Give yourself grace and remember what Grandma says: "Practice makes perfect!"

> *If then you were raised with Christ, seek those things which are above, where Christ is, sitting at the right hand of God.*
> *Set your mind on things above, not on things on the earth.*

Colossians 3:1-2 (NKJV)

Look at that action word—*Set.* It's a choice and plan.

> *Let the Spirit change your way of thinking.*

Ephesians 4:23 (CEV)

Take time to ask the Spirit to change you.

> *And do not be conformed to this world, but be transformed by the renewing of your mind, so that you may prove what the will of God is, that which is good and acceptable and perfect.*

Romans 12:2 (NKJV)

Renew...renew...renew!

Strategies to Move Us Forward

What are some strategies we use to reframe our hearts, minds, words, and actions?

Here is a great list the ladies in the webinar shared. (Thanks, Ladies!)

It's exciting to see how many we came up with:

1. Memorize and meditate on God's Word;
2. Commit to the task;
3. Be STILL before the Lord (Psalm 46:10);
4. Meditate on God's Word as we are commanded throughout scripture (Psalm 119:11);
5. Invite others to speak into your life - iron sharpens iron (Proverbs 27:17);
6. Ask yourself, "What do I need right now?";
7. Sing or listen to uplifting music;
8. Stop hitting the replay button;
9. Study the Word (2 Timothy 2:15);
10. Push the pause button in the busyness of life and life situations (Psalm 37:7);
11. Take a nature walk;
12. Take everything to God in prayer (Philippians 4:6);
13. Re-word our thinking from *I have to*, to *I get to*. Lay down the *shoulda, coulda, wouldas*;
14. Post His promises all over!
15. Choose an attitude of gratitude (1 Chronicles 16:34).

We Can Also Help Others Reframe Their Mindset

So, how can we help others reframe their hearts and minds? Is there anything we can do more specifically?

Yes, here are a few ways we can help our friends, family members, or business associates adjust their mindset when they are a bit off-kilter:

- Speak the truth in love. Use gentleness to restore or redirect (Ephesians 4:15).
- Answer with God's Word, not your opinion or advice.
- Pray they see the need for an adjustment to their mindset.
- Connect and empathize. We tend to want to make it better by saying things like...."*at least.....*". But we can't fix it. However, we can say, "*This stinks. I'm so glad you shared this with me.*"

When someone shares something off-base, I often jokingly say, "Where is that found in the Bible? Oh, that's right! 1 Nowhere 1:1." Then they laugh and realize their thoughts aren't correctly aligned with the Truth. As you can see, sometimes the things we believe, think, or say to ourselves are not found in scripture.

And be careful of false framing. It's when we frame something differently than it is. It's the equivalent of putting up a picture from the store with the manufacturer's picture in the frame. It may look good, but it is not your family or your picture.

It is important to be real and transparent,
as it can help others when they are struggling, too.

Other things to remember:

- Check in with body signals; they can inform us of our thoughts and emotions if we are ignoring something, are distracted, or get too busy.
- Life and death are in the power of the tongue (Proverbs 18:21).
- Be mindful of our words to self and others—spoken and written.

- Speak the truth in love (Ephesians 4:15).
- Heed the prompting of the Holy Spirit (John 16:13).
- Stay away from taking offense, comparing, or assuming.
- Change the channel or shift gears when needed.
- Make wise choices, with confidence (Matthew 6:33).

As you can see, reframing is needed in all of our lives. Sometimes it is a small adjustment and sometimes it is a large move.

Just a little reframing helps us see the real picture. In this case, it is still me.

Reframe Your Mindset

Better yet:

REFRAME with Jesus continually and you will know that your mindset is framed correctly every time.

Chapter 7

Maintaining God-Confidence in Warfare: The Power of Remembering

Yerinita T. Curtis-Fuller

For the weapons of our warfare are not carnal, but mighty through God to the pulling down of strongholds; Casting down imaginations, and every high thing that exalteth itself against the knowledge of God and bringing into captivity every thought to the obedience of Christ.

2 Corinthians 10:4-5 (KJV)

- Are the weapons you're using the ones God desires you to fight with?
- Did you leave your confidence in the last battle?
- Is He a God of the past and not a NOW God?

What is Spiritual Warfare?

Are the weapons you are using those God desires you to fight with?

There's a war that takes place in the heavenlies and manifests in the earth of good versus evil. Satan wages war against disciples of Jesus Christ consistently and relentlessly. Satan uses his wicked devices against us as believers in order to cause us to succumb and give up on our walk of faith. The enemy even uses people to carry out his wicked schemes. The Bible tells us,

For we are not fighting against flesh-and-blood enemies, but against evil rulers and authorities of the unseen world, against mighty powers in this dark world, and against evil spirits in the heavenly places.

Ephesians 6:12 (NLT)

I believe many of us don't understand that Satan is waging war, and we are in it. The Bible calls these attacks the *wiles of the devil* and explains them in detail. So, what are the wiles of the devil? They are evil and wicked schemes, attacks, methods, and strategies designed to deceive the believer. These things are also designed to ensnare, cause fear and intimidation. If we are not careful to use our weapons of warfare, Satan could win his battle against us.

What are our weapons of warfare? The Word of God, and the Name and the Blood of Jesus Christ. Notice how our Lord and Savior Jesus Christ responded to the enemy in Luke, chapter 4:1-13, NLT.

The Temptation of Jesus

> Then Jesus, full of the Holy Spirit, returned from the Jordan River. He was led by the Spirit in the wilderness, where he was tempted by the devil for forty days. Jesus ate nothing all that time and became very hungry.
>
> Then the devil said to him, "If you are the Son of God, tell this stone to become a loaf of bread." But Jesus told him, "No! The scriptures say, 'People do not live by bread alone.'"
>
> Then the devil took him up and revealed to him all the kingdoms of the world in a moment of time. "I will give you the glory of these kingdoms and authority over them," the devil said, "because they are mine to give to anyone I please. I will give it all to you if you will worship me."
>
> Jesus replied, "The scriptures say, 'You must worship the Lord your God and serve only him.'"
>
> Then the devil took him to Jerusalem, to the highest point of the Temple, and said, "If you are the Son of God, jump off! For the scriptures say, 'He will order his angels to protect and guard you. And they will hold you up with their hands so you won't even hurt your foot on a stone.'"

Jesus responded, "The scriptures also say, 'You must not test the Lord your God.' "

When the devil had finished tempting Jesus, he left him until the next opportunity came.

Here we see Jesus defeating the devil with what is written in the Word of God. If the weapon of the Word worked for Him, why wouldn't it work for us? Shouldn't we be doing what Jesus did in order to win the war every single time? Isn't our God-confidence found in the Lord showing us that if we do things His way, it is a sure VICTORY?

We are commanded to put on the whole armor of God in order to stand against the wiles of the devil. What is this armor?

Stand therefore, having girded your waist with truth, having put on the breastplate of righteousness, and having shod your feet with the preparation of the gospel of peace; above all, taking the shield of faith with which you will be able to quench all the fiery darts of the wicked one. And take the helmet of salvation, and the sword of the Spirit, which is the word of God; praying always with all prayer and supplication in the Spirit, being watchful to this end with all perseverance and supplication for the saints, Ephesians 6:14-18 (NKJV).

So again, I reiterate, what do we have to fear concerning spiritual warfare? Absolutely NOTHING. God has prepared, equipped and trained us to stand against the devil. He has given us spiritual armor to protect us in this battle versus good and evil. God has given us the assurance of His presence in this verse, *Do not be afraid or terrified because of them, for the Lord your God goes with you; he will never leave you or forsake you* (Deuteronomy 31:6 NKJV).

Finally, in Joshua 1:9 (NLT) He has commanded us to be strong and courageous in the midst of warfare. *So do not throw away this confident trust in the Lord. Remember the great reward it brings you!* (Hebrews 10:35 NLT).

Regardless of what it looks like in the natural, we as believers are on the winning side. Be confident in this.

Did you leave your confidence in the last battle?

We know that confidence is faith in God, certainty, and assurance of one's relationship with God. This confidence gives us a sense of boldness that is not dependent upon our own strength but the strength of God.

God accomplishes what we cannot do in our own strength.

Author Unknown

In order to be confident, we must know that we are fully accepted by God and that our victories depend upon Him. I would say that confidence is complete surrender and trust in the ways and character of God. I call it a blessed assurance. Of course, confidence of this magnitude is built over time and through the personal experiences we have with God.

We learn about Bible characters who walked by faith in fierce battles and overcame them by the power of God, but there comes a time when God wants to reveal His power to us on a personal level. How does God do this? By allowing us to go through experiences that include trials and tribulation that will build our trust, faith, and confidence in Him.

I would say that confidence is complete surrender and trust in the ways and character of God.

The Bible tells us to, *Consider it pure joy, my brothers and sisters, whenever you face trials of many kinds, because you know that the testing of your faith produces steadfastness. And let steadfastness have its full effect, that you may be perfect and complete, lacking nothing* (James 1:2-4, NIV). There is also a verse in Hebrews that says, *Patient endurance is what you need now, so that you will continue to do God's will. Then you will receive all that he has promised* (Hebrews 10:36 NLT).

Some of us may have cultivated confidence in the Lord but something happened that caused us to throw away our confidence. Some of us left our confidence in the last battle because it looked like we had lost.

Allow me to share a personal example.

I am a woman of prayer who has truly seen miracles, signs, and wonders happen right before my eyes. I have seen miracles happen for others as I interceded on their behalf. Well, a few years ago my husband became very ill, and he transitioned to his eternal home even after I prayed fervently for him to live. I remember coming boldly to the throne of grace in my time of need. I had no fear of him dying, I knew that He would overcome. I stood over Him interceding to no avail. God called Him home. My confidence was crushed. Didn't I pray by faith? Was doubt present as I prayed? Should I have prayed longer and more fervently? Was there anything else I could do to stop this from happening?

My confidence in the Lord was shattered, but not for long. I realized that my will for my husband couldn't prevail against the will of God. My husband's transition had nothing to do with a lack of faith in God. It had nothing to do with how I prayed or how long I prayed. I couldn't change this, I had to accept it.

Can you relate to my story? Did you pray for something, and it didn't go the way you had desired? Did you lose your confidence in the last battle? Did the hurt and pain cause you to question your ability to trust in the Lord again? If so, there is still hope for you. You can gain confidence in the Lord by accepting what didn't happen and focusing on what did.

What do I mean? **There is power in remembering.**

You must remember the prior victories the Lord gave you before so your confidence in Him will be restored. I did grieve my loss, and I still do to this very moment, but my perspective is different. I could not throw away all the miracles, signs and wonders I had seen before the loss of my dear husband.

I simply began to REMEMBER the Lord's goodness towards me and my children.

My song became, "Lord you are good, and I will see your goodness again in the land of the living."

There is POWER IN REMEMBERING.

I remembered how God healed me from a serious condition. I remembered when God healed my daughter of seizures. I remembered when God provided, protected, and comforted us as we walked through a wilderness experience. I remembered the days when it seemed like all hope was lost as we lost our possessions and lost relationships we thought would last a lifetime. I remembered God's constant faithfulness towards us and my heart cried out, *'God causes everything to work together for the good of those who love Him and are called according to His purpose for them'* (Romans 8:28, NLT). My song became, *Lord you are good, and I will see your goodness again in the land of the living.* As I watched my children grieve their father, I constantly reminded myself, and them, that everything was going to be alright.

How can I say this during grief and what we are currently facing right now?

I *choose* to still believe in God no matter what. I *choose* to maintain God-confidence through it all—and so can you. Job said, *Though he slay me, yet will I trust in him:...* (Job 13:15 KJV).

Will you join me in trusting Him again and thus regain your confidence?

There is POWER IN REMEMBERING.

Asaph knew the importance of remembering to gain back his confidence during warfare. He said in his distress, *I think of the good old days, long since ended, when my nights were filled with joyful songs. I search my soul and ponder the difference now,* Psalm 77:5-6, NLT. He goes on to say, *...this is my fate; the Most High has turned his hand against me. But then I recall all you have done, O Lord; I remember your wonderful deeds of long ago. They are* *constantly in my thoughts. I cannot stop thinking about your mighty works* (Psalm 77:10-12).

This same God equipped David who confidently faced Goliath as He remembered that God had allowed him to kill a lion and a bear with his bare hands. David placed all his confidence in the Lord to take off the head of a giant that no one else wanted to face. The Lord had the people of Israel set up stones of remembrance in Joshua 4:9 (NKJV) so that they wouldn't forget His miracles. He remembered Hannah's cry and allowed her to give birth to a son after years of being tormented by Peninnah in 1 Samuel 1:19. The three Hebrew boys had confidence that the Lord would deliver them from the fiery furnace in Daniel 3.

There is POWER IN REMEMBERING.

In conclusion, what should we remember in times of spiritual warfare? And what are the benefits of remembering?

- We must remember the character of God and that He keeps His word.
- We must remember prior victories.
- We must remember that God is the same today, yesterday and forever.
- We must remember His faithfulness and goodness towards us.
- We must remember that no matter what it looks like, God is with us.
- We must remember that God loves us.

What are the benefits of remembering?

- Our faith, courage and hope are restored.
- Our strength, peace and comfort are restored.
- Our perspective, vision and mission are restored.
- Our focus, expectancy and peace are restored.
- Our worship and thanksgiving are restored.
- Our God-confidence is restored.

I leave you with the following scriptures that will truly bless your heart and help to restore and maintain God-confidence in spiritual warfare.

But blessed are those who trust in the Lord and have made the Lord their hope and confidence.

Jeremiah 17:7 (NLT)

Though a mighty army surrounds me, my heart will not be afraid. Even if I am attacked, I will remain confident.

Psalm 27:3 (NLT)

And this righteousness will bring peace. Yes, it will bring quietness and confidence forever.

Isaiah 32:17 (NLT)

And I am certain that God, who began the good work within you, will continue his work until it is finally finished on the day when Christ Jesus returns.

Philippians 1:6 (NIV)

The same God who delivered us then will deliver us now.

Yerinita (Nita) T. Curtis Fuller is an author, speaker, mentor and life coach who has dedicated her life to helping people find their purpose, endure life's challenges and teaching them to maintain healthy and thriving relationships. She is founder of Purposed Pursuits Life Coaching, LLC and has served as keynote speaker at many conferences, workshops, and life groups.

Yerinita has had her share of life's difficulties. She has overcome childhood traumas, health issues, and broken relationships. Yerinita is also persevering after the sudden loss of her husband of twenty-six years. She is known for her strong faith and ability to endure any situation she encounters.

For nearly fifteen years Yerinita has enjoyed walking in her purpose. She is passionate about supporting, encouraging, and inspiring change. She has learned through life's ups and downs the importance of walking in your destiny, loving others, and demonstrating compassion towards all. Yerinita believes that no one should walk alone in times of transition. She is a voice of hope to all who are seeking a change of course and believes that opportunities to support others are endless.

Purposed Pursuits Life Coaching, LLC was birthed with a vision to provide help to individuals and couples who are truly ready for transformation. The mission is to provide individuals with the necessary tools to navigate through life's difficulties and come to the realization that it's never too late to achieve your dreams. Purposed Pursuits Life Coaching, LLC. stands behind the truth that "There is purpose for every life, directions for every path, and solutions to every problem."

https://purposedpursuitsllc.org

Chapter 8

Finding a Crown of Confidence … Once Again

Niki Banning

"For I know the plans I have for you," says the Lord. "They are plans for good and not for disaster, to give you a future and a hope."

Jeremiah 29:11 (NLT)

- Are you feeling lost and alone, and have you lost your confidence? Are you wondering where to find confidence once again?
- Have you experienced those dreaded days (or even weeks!) when you can't find your crown? Or does your crown need readjusting?
- Has life thrown you a curveball, and shaken your confidence? Are you wondering how to get your confidence back on track?

Of Crowns and Fuzzy Socks

Most days, you'll find me in my cozy office, decked out in sweat-pants and a Zoom-appropriate top—just in case. And always sporting a pair of fuzzy socks. With eternally cold toes, I never forget my socks.

Yet, even though I'm a daughter of the Most High King, some days - I forget to put on my crown.

You see, I've been pondering confidence. Where *do* I look for my own confidence, *who is it* that fills those empty spaces in me—and *why on earth* does this seem to be a struggle, especially for those of us who are Christ-followers?

Let me take you back to early June 2021.

At a Loss for Confidence

We made a cross-country move from Missouri to Arizona. We're certainly not the only family who has ever packed up an entire house (complete with an unhappy teenager in tow!) and trekked miles away from familiarity and comfort.

But this? This move added a whole other level of angst and chal-lenges for our family. It brought on emotional crises for my teenage daughter Chase, growing pains in my virtual assistant business (lovely and uncomfortable at the same time!), and difficulties and distance in my marriage. On top of that, the guilt and pain of sepa-ration from my two adult kiddos, Peyton and Kenna, who remained in Missouri, took my breath away time and again.

My confidence? Well. That went right out the window.

Now, don't get me wrong. We had some fun times, despite the con-stant distress, which felt ever-present. One of the reasons for our move to Arizona was to be nearer to my oldest daughter Josie and my two precious (and rather precocious!) granddaughters, Zoey and Addy. Spending time with them was a bright spot for us when things felt hard.

But here's the thing. When God threw the doors wide open and asked us to be faithful in our move to Arizona, He never promised it would be a walk in the proverbial park—**but what He did promise is that He would be there every step of the way.**

Now, Where Did I Leave That Crown?

There were days—even weeks—that seemed I would never pull out from under the heavy weight: new routines, loneliness, a teenager in despair, and communication breakdown within our four walls. Our lives seemed to move from crisis to crisis, never allowing me to come up for air. Yet I could hear God's faintest whisper, 'I'm still here,' and I would obediently reach for my crown.

But some days, I just couldn't seem to find that crown, no matter how hard I tried.

Those days when I was overwhelmed with my own sadness, the pain and grief my daughter carried, and the growing indifference at home, I felt that just maybe the crown had been packed away, hidden in a box of memories, or deep inside a closet somewhere. Maybe that box would never see the light of day again.

Oh, there were positives to be found. We didn't move across the country and only find disappointments. In the midst of the journey, my virtual assistant business grew, even flourished. God flung the doors wide open for me. I was blessed. Slightly overwhelmed and maybe even a little discombobulated with all the new things to learn—but *so* very blessed. It was a beautiful distraction, yet a way for me to pour into others and begin to see my purpose once again.

Rob's new job was what he'd always wanted. He worked with family, his income increased, and he managed fewer folks. That's an all-around win! But it also came with sacrifice, as his long daily commute and very early morning hours took a toll on him physically and mentally and, ultimately, on our relationship. I wondered if we would ever get back to where we had been before the move.

Chase found a new dance studio to call home (5-6 days per week at dance equals a second home, after all) and began to thrive there. Her new school began on a positive note but quickly soured into cliques and mean girls—and boys, for that matter. It all added to the tremendous stress she was already carrying.

Nothing felt *right* anymore. It was all upside down and full of tension. I longed for the familiarity of our previous home and the comfort of family and close friends.

Rediscovering My Crown

So, what exactly was a Missouri girl to do while feeling lost and alone in Arizona? I put on my favorite fuzzy socks, determined to find my crown—and sought my Father's heart once again. Where had I lost sight of whose I am and where my confidence lies?

It was in one of those moments of deep pain, disconnect, and loneliness that I heard Him speak to me, oh so clearly, *'Child, lift your head.'* His presence was tangible. It wrapped around me like a warm fuzzy blanket, bringing a sense of peace and comfort that I hadn't known in months.

I cracked open my Bible again and read afresh the verses that had carried me through times of stress and distress in years past.

My life verse, Jeremiah 29:11, ran through my head. *For I know the plans I have for you. ... Good plans ... plans to give you a hope and a future.* There it was—and it was there all along. I had to rediscover the truth within those words. Jesus was my anchor, the calm in my storm. I only needed to hold fast to Him and His promises. He put that reminder in front of me countless times. My sister Kim encouraged me to hold tight to my anchor. My pastor spoke about our anchor in Christ. Friends and devotionals spoke confirmation. OK, Lord! I get it!

Jesus is your anchor, the calm in your storm.
You only need to hold fast to Him and His promises.

It is better to take refuge in the Lord
than to trust in people.

Psalm 118:8 (NLT)

Psalms 118:8 gently reminded me that my confidence comes from Him, not from my circumstances or anyone around me. I was able to look at my marriage and my husband with a refreshed heart, relying on God, rather than Rob, for my confidence— and our marriage began to heal.

> *Don't be afraid, for I am with you.*
> *Don't be discouraged, for I am your God.*
> *I will strengthen you and help you.*
> *I will hold you up with my victorious right hand.*
>
> Isaiah 41:10 (NLT)

The Lord led me to Isaiah 41:10. His promise to hold me up was daily in my thoughts, thereby earning a spot on the verse wall in my office. He strengthened and upheld me; He held me up with His righteous right hand.

Knowing He was holding me, and my family, freed me from the weight I had been carrying for so long. **It was never mine to carry.**

I could finally see with new eyes and feel His confidence growing in me again.

Finding My Crown

Through my physical journey from Missouri to Arizona, and most certainly my emotional journey toward renewed confidence in the Lord, I came to know once again that God was indeed with me through it all. He walked me through the transitions of my daily life and relationships, even as I stumbled. I found my crown, albeit not very gracefully most days, as I looked to Him, surrendered, and trusted in His will.

Has it been rainbows and sunshine since those days of finding my crown again? I'd love to give an enthusiastic *Yes!* But alas, there are days when I still have to go searching.

But through it all, His hand guides, leads, and comforts. On the challenging days, I seek Him and regain that confidence yet again. I may be in my fuzzy socks, and my crown may be crooked—but I know I am loved and held by my unchanging, unfailing Anchor.

This hope is a strong and trustworthy anchor for our souls.
It leads us through the curtain into God's inner sanctuary.

Hebrews 6:19 (NLT)

Niki Banning is a Jesus-loving mom, wife, and Yaya.

By day, she has been blessed to see her Virtual Assistant practice blossom since moving from Missouri to Arizona in 2021. She had a decade of office management experience in the financial services industry before moving into the world of entrepreneurship.

By night, she has found a reignited passion for writing and is a newly-minted author as part of a collaborative book and the new Associate Director of RHEMA Publishing House.

Through involvement first as a Caregiver, and then as a leader in Stephen Ministry, Niki found her passion and calling—to serve and come alongside others in support.

Niki is a relationship-builder, encourager, and ally. She has been blessed with the ability to help others calm the chaos of their business and be a trusted partner and right hand.

You can find Niki in her office, wearing fuzzy socks, and accompanied by her also-fuzzy office dogs, Otto and Ruby.

https://nikibvirtualservices.com

Chapter 9

Confidence in Finances:
Stewardship vs. Ownership

Kim Smith

*But seek ye first the kingdom of God, and his righteousness;
and all these things shall be added unto you.*
Matthew 6:33 (KJV)

- Have you ever felt confident about your finances?
- What keeps you from feeling confident about your finances?
- If you gained control of your finances, how could you change someone's life and family legacy with your gifts?

How Is Your Heart Feeling about Money?

Money is not the most exciting topic for most people, but if we handle it God's way, it can become an exciting part of our life.
Billy Graham so aptly said, "If a person gets their attitude toward money straight, it will help straighten out almost every other area in their life."

Perspective—God wants ours to be like His.

It's not about how much we have at this moment, it's about how we currently handle what God has entrusted to us. He is willing and able to pour out blessing upon blessing, not only financial ones, when we obediently steward what He's already placed in our hands. He wants to bless us, but we need to be in a position for Him to do that.

Whether we're a mom, a wife, a business owner, a community leader, an entrepreneur, a ministry leader, or in a leadership position at work, it's likely we have some input related to money. Folks, it flows from the top down. If we're not doing well with our money, it's affecting others—or at least, other areas of our lives.

Gaining Confidence through Stewardship

Has the Holy Spirit been talking to you about your finances lately? In talking with many people over the years, I have found shame and guilt and a lack of education and teaching related to finances are significant contributors to why many lack confidence in this area.

One way to gain confidence is to become debt free. Can you fathom being debt free? Paying for nothing but your essentials. What would it do for you? What would it do for *your* confidence?

My sister learned a surprising lesson about confidence when she was 14. As she recalls:

> Middle school is *such* a hard time to be a girl! But, something I can remember oh so clearly is that *one* outfit that made me feel *more than confident*. You see, growing up, we didn't have much money. In fact, Mom had to budget on a shoestring just to outfit my brother, sisters, and me each school year. She loved thrifting, hand-me-downs, and garage sales. Out of sheer embarrassment, I used to hide on the car floorboard when she pulled up to any type of sale.
>
> Just before my eighth-grade year, Mom took me to JCPenney to go shopping. "Look for the pink tags," she said. For all the younger folks reading, pink tags meant "clearance" at that time. Going to

an actual department store was a *treat*. When I found that mint-green, multi-color striped sweater and those navy pants (stay with me here, it was the 80s…) on that clearance rack, I was in *heaven*. I felt like a million bucks on Mom's shoestring budget.

And let me tell you—every single time I wore that outfit to school, someone complimented my style. Little did they know my hand-me-down, thrift store, and garage sale backstories. But boy, did I gain confidence that year. I will never, ever forget my trip to JCPenney, my Mom's budget, and especially—that sweater and those pants. And I'm forever grateful.

Scripture tells us it's all His: our money, possessions, health, and all that we have.

This vital lesson applies to all of us. When it comes to our money as believers, it's easy to get our perspective shifted to the world's perception of "our" money. Scripture tells us it's all His. We may have difficulty wrapping our minds around this fact; we work for it, so how can it all be His? Isn't what we give to church His?

We may forget, but the way we handle our finances in our business correlates to how we handle them in our personal lives and vice versa.

It's all about Stewardship

"The definition of *steward* in the Bible lends itself to the idea of an 'overseer' or 'manager' over someone else's matters."[1]

In Genesis 15:2, the original Hebrew word for "steward" is `albayith, which literally means "man over the house." During Bible times, most notable households would have had a steward, so the term was familiar and not originally tied to spiritual matters. The steward might be in charge of the master's possessions.

A steward is one who manages or looks after another's property or matters, a caretaker of God's kingdom. As an owner, we can do anything we want with our stuff, but as a steward, we give account to the owner for what we do with his stuff.

Pedro Adao, Founder of The 100X Academy, says, "It's a high calling to care for another's property. We're wired to take care of other people's stuff."[2]

Lord means owner. Jesus can't be our Lord and owner if we don't do what He wants, or don't want what He wants.

> *The earth is the LORD's, and everything in it,*
> *the world, and all who live in it...*
> Psalm 24:1 (NIV)

Stewardship vs. Ownership

Stewardship is actually a higher calling than ownership because we're managing another person's possessions for them. We are doing this for the highest and best interest of another. And as believers, we are stewarding everything God gives us and that is important for the kingdom. **If we're not keeping account, we're technically not stewarding.**

> *But remember the LORD your God, for it is he who gives you*
> *the ability to produce wealth, and so confirms his covenant,*
> *which he swore to your ancestors, as it is today.*
> Deuteronomy 8:18 (NIV)

As we know, it is all God's and HE is the one who gives gifts, produces wealth, and showers blessings.

Confidence is Tied to Hope

When we know whose money it really is and the job He's called us to regarding it, our confidence begins to grow. The word confidence is tied to hope, and it means trust, belief, assurance, certainty, courage, a spirit of determination. On the other hand, the antonyms for confidence are doubt, insecurity, self-doubt, uncertainty.

When we're stewarding God's way, confidence is a natural byproduct. Stewarding brings confidence, which brings freedom. This goes beyond freedom in our finances. This freedom starts to impact other areas of our lives.

Stewarding what we already have prepares us for more. We can only steward what we've been entrusted with, so how are we currently stewarding what we've been given? Our nature is to want more…more stuff, more money, more house, better cars, and the list goes on. If we are living like this, can God entrust us with more? Like the parable of the talents in Matthew 25:14-20, Jesus is looking to see how we're doing with what He's already blessed us.

Tell Your Money Where to Go

Many things often keep us from feeling confident in the area of money and then we get stuck on the hamster wheel. Some of them include past financial decisions, more month than money, money fights, and buyer's remorse. Sometimes life happens and cars break down, people get sick, companies downsize, and disasters strike—even when we are handling money correctly. But proper stewarding makes these challenges so much easier.

Confidence comes from being intentional and handling money God's way. He infuses confidence in us and causes it to increase when we follow His instructions.

We all have a money story. Mine changed my life so much, it created a life-long passion to help others manage their money well. Like you, I had to learn how to tell my money what to do to manage it well. It's about you telling your money what to do and increasing confidence; it's not about allowing money to control you, because that diminishes confidence.

If we're in bondage to our finances via bank loans, credit card debt, student loans, and furniture loans, often we aren't able to give the way we'd like to. Our confidence in God and our ability to practice generosity or start that business He's laid on our heart is diminished because the funds are not available for those things.

Sometimes we have an idea of how we'd like our finances to look, but no one can tell us how to get to where we want to go financially unless we know where we are now. If you don't know where you stand currently, it's likely you don't have a plan or know how to get to where you want to be.

That's not profound, but it is practical. Similar to traveling, you have to have a map and know where you are now to figure out how to get to the place you want to go. In order to elevate and be free from poverty and bondage, we must become good stewards of the resources He has already given us.

Do:

There are several ways to do this.

Do set a budget, save for emergencies, and plan for retirement. These are ways of being diligent and planning ahead. Planning ahead builds confidence.

Don't:

Don't accumulate debt. You can't borrow your way out of debt, and debt makes you a slave.

My Story

Let me share my story to illustrate how our past affects our lives and financial future, for the good and the bad.

I think I realized at a very young age the responsibility of being a firstborn could be both a blessing and a curse. My early childhood was uneventful, and I never thought that my family wouldn't always look the way it did during those early years.

When I was 5-8 years old and played wiffle ball with my dad and friends, my dad would pick my friends to be on his team and would let them go first in what seemed like every game we played. This painful rejection deeply affected my self-esteem and identity. I think it caused me to seek approval and created a need to be perfect from a young age. I always wanted to do things right and not mess up. I created tough, hard-to-live-up-to standards, and I didn't want to disappoint others, either.

Against my will and much to my dismay, when I was in fifth grade, our family moved from the city to the country.

Less than a year later, when I was 12, just after our family of six moved into our newly built home, my dad left our family for our neighbor from the city. My world turned upside down the afternoon my dad pulled me out of recess to tell me he was leaving because, as he said, "I no longer love your mother." What in the world? I was taught that marriage was for good. I remember wanting my dad's approval, yet at the same time being bitter at him for leaving us. My baby sister was five months old, and mom had never worked outside the home, but it was clear that to support her four kids she would have to get a job, other than being a stay-at-home mom. It was October when he left. The next three months were hard emotionally, and providing for our physical needs became nearly impossible for our mom. I suddenly became, as Mom has often said, "her right-hand man"—or woman, in this case. I helped potty train my youngest sister and cared for my three siblings after school most days.

At Christmastime that year, I experienced two of the greatest moments that have impacted my life. How crazy to think that at age 12, and now over 40 years later, they still direct my purpose and passion in life.

We weren't going hungry, but I remember we had been eating beans and rice, lots of peanut butter & jelly, and pancakes. Again, it was Christmastime and Mom told us she was behind on house payments and could no longer afford to keep the house—and we would have to move in with my aunt several hours away. I had lots of friends, and because of our recent move, I really didn't want to move again—and I begged God that we could stay where we were.

In a different way than I would have ever imagined, God answered that prayer.

Right before Christmas, on a dark evening, the doorbell rang and Mom opened it to find some men from church on our doorstep with a furniture box filled with food. Not only were they welcomed, but also *greatly* appreciated. Without a doubt, that is the Christmas—of all my years—I remember most. This was my first recollection of God providing for my needs. As I grew older, I remember recognizing it wasn't by chance those folks came together to provide for our needs; they had a heart *and* an ability to give. They were the body of Christ coming together to provide for a single mom and her kids. God had not only provided for our needs but He had impressed me with the example of giving.

Near that same time, my mom called the bank and said to Mr. Banker, "I'm unable to keep the home, and I'm going to have to give it back to the bank." The banker informed her someone had paid the last four months of house payments and the real estate taxes that were due. It still brings tears to my eyes to know someone was prompted and listened to the call to step up to the plate on our behalf. Their giving had a profound impact on my life, and I hoped someday I could do that for someone else. In a recent conversation, it was brought up that we could have been homeless—not necessarily living on the streets—but not having a home of our own. But God! By the way, my mom and step-dad live in that same house 40 plus years later.

Within a few years of my parents' divorce, I became a teen mom during my junior year in high school. Being the responsible firstborn I am, I got married within three weeks of finding out I was pregnant.

Married life was not rosy, but I chose to honor the commitment I had made. I learned in those early years with my husband working in construction how to stretch a dollar and to budget in my own way so that we weren't constantly in crisis. While in my twenties, I helped friends and family clear up bad debts so they could buy a house, grocery shop better, menu plan, and just do better with their money. Those things came naturally for me, and I found the challenges invigorating and fun.

When I was in my early twenties, I had a life-changing conversation with a friend who told me she and her husband had built one house, sold it, and were doing it two more times—and then would be debt free. I had no idea what that really meant and was clueless how someone did not owe anyone for anything—not even their house! However, it was so intriguing to me that I was hungry to know more. She told me to listen to Larry Burkett on the radio. Such a simple thing, but an additional life-changing experience for me. We started doing some of the things he suggested and seeing small wins along the way. We already paid cash for cars, and I wondered how there could be anything else I could possibly change to improve our financial situation. One of the very small things we did was to apply my husband's 10-cent an hour raise to our mortgage because, after all, we were "already making it." Unless there was a true need, every month we added it to our mortgage payment. Little-by-little, we were seeing that debt number eke down.

By my late twenties, I realized and even noted on paper at the beginning of one year, one of my personal goals was to help people with their money. I didn't know what that would look like, but it was important to me.

In my early thirties, though I lagged behind with fear and trepidation, my husband decided to go into business for himself. Being in construction was truly a feast or famine lifestyle, so we didn't want to live in a constant roller coaster state with our finances. But, because we'd been living with a plan, within five months of that decision, we became completely debt free. We did this weird thing of paying double and triple principal each month to make real headway.

Maybe you recall, the years between 1999 and 2008 were plentiful with construction. We did well, enjoyed life, ate out when we wanted to, paid for our daughter's college education, AND took on $400,000 of real estate debt. In our minds, real estate debt wasn't nearly as bad as consumer debt. In reality, it didn't matter if it was real estate or consumer debt, it still had our name on it.

In 2007, I had the opportunity to lead Dave Ramsey's Financial Peace University (aka FPU) classes. I was excited to teach concepts we had already implemented, as well as learn some new things along the way.

Then came 2008. The recession knocked the wind out of us in our construction business, along with the weight of carrying all that debt. Our income had increased steadily from 2004-2008, but suddenly it all changed. Here I was leading financial classes and teaching all these principles, yet carrying the burden of our own debt load. We decided it was time to knuckle down and get debt free *again*. Part of that decision included not eating out, going on vacations, or spending unnecessarily. We seemed boring to those around us, but we had a goal—to get out of debt as soon as possible and not incur debt again. During the next four and a half years, we had a couple of things that didn't change in our plan. We continued to tithe, give above our tithe, and pay for our son's education. We wondered if we would be able to make those tuition payments till he graduated. For us, those were commitments we resolved to make happen.

You'd be surprised how many people fear thinking they'll have to sacrifice *everything* to become debt free or attain the goals they dream about. Yes, it's hard, and you will have to make some sacrifices; but YOU get to decide what's most important to YOU.

We spent four-and-a-half years not doing things perfectly but busting our tails to break free of the bondage of debt. On November 13th, 2014, the night before our twin granddaughters were born, we made the final payment on the $400,000 of debt. I kept thinking as I handed the check over to the bank that they should be shooting off fireworks, or at least congratulating and celebrating with us. That didn't happen though, because they weren't nearly as happy as we were to be rid of that debt.

Some months later, we were able to take our granddaughter with us to be on Dave Ramsey's radio program for a "debt free scream!" At five years old, she loved being able to yell, "We're debt free!" with us. For us, it not only gave us the opportunity to share our accomplishment with the world, but more importantly, to share with her the legacy of being debt free. We were influencing lives beyond our own.

Yes, my responsibility trait showed up in good ways, but it equally had the tendency to keep things from being fun. Keeping focused on our goals was important, but we couldn't forget to enjoy the journey and do things that aligned with our long-term desires. Since that time, God has afforded us the ability to give and do some extraordinary things. In giving several thousand dollars toward the adoptions of a couple of families, we know we not only helped change their future but also influenced others to do the same. We give well above our tithe to many organizations that we are passionate about, and finally, most recently, we were able to purchase a 100 plus acre farm (after looking for approximately five years) to turn into a retreat venue, as well as a place for ours and our daughter's homes. The level of peace we experience and the ability to give spontaneously is actually contagious! Our perseverance, sacrifice, and goal-setting help us continue reaching our debt free dreams.

During the years of 2007-2012, while leading more than twelve Financial Peace University classes, I coached many people after class, sitting in McDonald's or at my dining room table. After attending training to lead our church through a church-wide program in 2011, our pastor agreed to let me oversee the program. You see, our church had taken on a $2.3 million building project debt in 2009 and he didn't want it hanging over our heads or holding back ministry. With my leadership overseeing 14 classes, over $213,000 of debt was paid off and approximately $175,000 was saved in nine weeks through roughly 250 people (singles & married). And I'm happy to announce our church paid off $2.3 million in nine years instead of 30. The people had to do the work and God brought the blessing.

Another client recently paid off number five of six student loans and said the peace of knowing she is more in control of her finances has made her more confident. Clients often tell me I help them feel comfortable talking about money—one of the most difficult conversations for many people.

You may be thinking, *Yeah, that's a nice story*, but it was a road filled with potholes and detours. If there's someone who understands not having all the pieces of a perfect life, I fit the bill. With my back story of getting married extremely young, my chances for success might have been laughed at.

Prioritizing With a Plan

Having confidence in your finances is not about giving up everything. It's about prioritizing with a plan.

Maybe you are intimidated by what you don't know about money, and you need someone to help you understand and walk this journey feeling equipped, empowered, and understanding how to live purposefully with both your life and money.

There I was, a preteen from a broken home, a teen mom and wife in a less than desirable, tumultuous marriage, making very little money. My story should inspire you. If I can tackle the debt monster and win, then so can you! Things that seem impossible can become possible.

We've made blunders along the way. But thankfully, we don't have to do this thing perfectly—and with God's grace, we can be overcomers.

We knew that God was on our side, and in the moments I was questioning whether we'd make it or not, both in marriage & with our money, He showed us He had other, greater things in store. Every day we walk by people not knowing their unique struggles. Remember—you can be free of debt and leave a legacy for your family, no matter how your situation looks now.

Most people walk by me and think I'm just your average American in debt and trying to keep up with the Joneses; but like the *Millionaire Next Door*, we're debt-free, saving, giving, and enjoying the benefits. It's not every day someone pays off $400,000 of debt and pays cash for 128 acres. I'm hopeful you can achieve these kinds of results, too.

The Trajectory of YOUR Life Can Change

The trajectory of my life changed when someone sacrificed for us so we could stay in our home—my family legacy changed. It gave my mom hope and confidence to be a warrior for us kids.

Whose life story or family tree is waiting to be changed as a result of you stewarding your money? God is waiting for you, and so are they. What if tomorrow it was your best friend or sister in need? Are you in a position to help without it being a strain on your home?

When we control our finances, the benefits are tremendous:

- When we learn better ways to handle our finances, we gain freedom and blessings beyond our imagination.
- When we can pay the bills without feeling overwhelmed or stretched, and when we have more money than month, our confidence grows.
- When we make a good purchase, are a generous or good steward, or bless someone and it doesn't put us in stress mode, our confidence grows.
- When we gain control of our finances, I propose we'll gain confidence in talking about money, knowing the best ways to give, and how to bless others without enabling.

Doing better in our finances may benefit us, but in God's reality and economy, it's likely to benefit someone else, too.

How on Earth do we Become Financially Free and Confident?

Seek Christ

> *But seek first the Kingdom of God and His righteousness and all these things shall be added unto you.*
> Matthew 6:33 (NKJV)

Ask God for Wisdom and then use it. James tells us to ask for it. Pray with a surrendered attitude.

Plan

Making a written plan helps us to look forward, and keeps us from drifting and spending all we make without thinking about the future—it's a form of accountability.

Careful planning puts you ahead in the long run;
hurry and scurry puts you further behind.

Proverbs 21:5 (MSG)

Budget

Create a way to save and spend based on what you have by naming every dollar. Again, tell your money where to go.

Prepare

Prepare for the unexpected; save for emergencies, such as car and home repairs, medical expenses, and other sudden events that come out of the blue.

A prudent person foresees danger and takes precautions.

Proverbs 27:12 (NLT)

Self-Control

Spending within your means, saving, and not jumping on to the next purchase are matters of self-control. Surrendering to God and walking in the fruit of the Spirit strengthens and brings about true self-control. And when you're operating your life and finances with self control, confidence naturally grows.

Serve Others

Step outside of yourself. Doing something kind for others changes your perspective, and your need for more diminishes. Help the needy, take someone a meal, give to a cause you believe in.

How you and I handle our finances affects God's Kingdom.

Read that again. ***How you and I handle our finances affects God's Kingdom***!

Are your finances aimlessly wandering, not getting you where you'd like to be; or are you feeling confident because you are stewarding well?

Gratitude and Contentment

Be content where you are and with what you have *right now.*

Be grateful for the ways God has already blessed you.

As a reminder, stewardship, a plan (aka budget), and obedience, bring blessing and favor that takes us higher and to places we often only dream of. Knowing that and having a grateful heart readies us to receive more. We save so we can sow. If we don't or can't save, we won't or can't sow.

God has a plan, and as imitators of God, it is wise to have a plan, knowing in the end He determines our steps.

> *A man's heart plans his way, But the Lord directs his steps.*
>
> Proverbs 16:9 (NKJV)

A plan tells you where you are, where you want to go, and outlines the steps to get there.

Stewardship is difficult, but…

    It is doable.
    It is possible.
    It is necessary.

Why Become Financially Free

When we are blessed, we can be a blessing. Take some time to read Robert Morris' book, 'The Blessed Life.' In it, he shares how he learned how to remarkably bless others with the money and resources God had given him.

There are tremendous benefits to becoming financially free, and this is just the beginning:

- We gain peace in finances and life;
- We can become generous givers who fund and expand the Kingdom;
- We reap the rewards of radical generosity;
- We have eternal impact;
- We pass on a legacy;
- We have less stress when the hard times come.

"We make a living by what we earn,
we make a life by what we give."
Winston Churchill

Confidence comes naturally when we're using wisdom, following God's Word, and doing what the Holy Spirit directs us to do.

Walking in confidence in our finances benefits us in our decision making. We don't have to make every decision under stress and duress. We can breathe and pause before we give our *yes* or *no*.

Additionally, we can now say yes to something we had to say no to previously, like a vacation, a furniture purchase, or helping provide for the adoption of a beautiful child into a family.

Remember to hold resources loosely; they are not truly ours. If God desires to do something with them differently from what we desire, we must not only be prepared for it but also be ready to follow through on what He directs. To surrender our resources to God, we must hold them with open hands as we lift them up to Him.

In my life, becoming debt free allowed me to help others in the Kingdom become debt free.

Debt free people create debt free churches that fund
Kingdom work in incredible ways.

Leaving a Godly Legacy

A good man leaves an inheritance for his children's children.
Proverbs 13:22 (NKJV)

This verse keeps our life goal, our vision, and our legacy front and center while we make plans for our money. God loves families and has woven legacy stories throughout the Bible. Bill High, founder of The Signatry, a global community and ministry dedicated to creating eternal impact through generosity across generations, said—*"God intends for families to have a lasting influence for generations. Giving together brings families together around common causes— serving others and doing good. Build a multi-generational legacy by shaping a family culture of celebration and generosity."* [3]

We must be intentional when it comes to stewarding our finances. Being intentional and following through will inevitably help our kids with good stewardship.

Would your kids know what to do (wisely) with a million dollars if you, or someone else, left it for them?

Pedro Adao said, "God wants to confront poverty & poverty mind-set in His people. It's keeping them from achieving their God-given destinies."[4]

Because opportunities are endless when it comes to funding King-dom work, we want to be people who pass on a legacy of faith and use our dollars to affect the Kingdom through impact and influence.

Another Legacy Story

Let me share a legacy story that changed a young man's financial future forever.

A few years ago, as a mom was looking through her safe, she stumbled upon a check box, the kind that checks come in when we order them in the mail. On the top of the box was a note labeled "rent." Four years prior, during her son's college years, while he was working and going to school, he paid a small weekly rent to her, and it piled up in the little box. The plan had been for the mom to secretly save it to give to him when he married.

Years later, the young man was the victim of theft and lost his business trailer and tools, so she decided it was the perfect time to bless him with this surprise money. When she called him to tell him about the saved money, he was shocked. Together, they guessed it might be $1,800, maybe $2,000. When she counted it and called him to share the actual amount, before sending it, he guessed several times and came nowhere close. To everyone's surprise, it was $6,000! By this time, this young man knew the value of money, what was stolen from him, and how God had replaced it. She sent her son the savings, and he decided to selflessly pay off his wife's vehicle, buy some tools to replace stolen ones, and then to give his three employees Christmas bonuses.

I am this proud Momma!

I cry every time I think of how *my son* wisely used some of his blessing to carry on the financial legacy that God had been instilling in us by blessing others.

We all can be recipients of a ripple effect,
but we can also be people who create ripples
that multiply throughout our homes, community and the world.

As you can see, to have generational impact, we must break the chains of financial bondage and become free.

Dave Ramsey, founder of Financial Peace University[5], often asks, "Do your kids have the bones of character to carry the blessing when you leave them with a million or more?"

A gifted financial coach can teach you good financial principles and how to handle money, but if you don't believe or apply those principles, they won't help you manage your money and build wealth.

A worthy goal in handling our finances and money is to be the kind of people who can carry the weight of financial blessing.

With God on our side and confidence in stewarding finances His way, we *can* create ripples of freedom for generational change.

You, I mean Y.O.U., can be a hope conduit, and so much more, for generations to come. Will you? He's waiting!

> *Live a life worthy of the calling you have received.*
> Ephesians 4:1 (NIV)

Endnotes

1. By Gina Calvert https://vision2.com/what-is-definition-of-steward-in-bible/

2 & 4. Pedro Adao, 31-Day Challenge https://www.31daywisdomchallenge.com/2023-wisdom

3. https://thesignatry.com

5. Dave Ramsey, Financial Peace Universtiy ramseysolutions.com

---

Kim has been married for nearly 39 years, is a mom to two adult children, and Granny to six. Kim inspires hope through relatable stories and is a catalyst for creating ripples of freedom as a Financial and Business & Legacy Coach.

Her heart's desire is to see families, businesses, and ultimately churches free from the debt that holds them back in so many ways.

A little over one year ago she accomplished a God-given dream when she launched a farmhouse vacation rental and retreat venue, Vossel Valley Farm Lakehouse and Loft.

As a coach in finances, business, leadership, and legacy, Kim can help you give every dollar a name, figure out the best plan for you or your business, plan for the future, and reach your goals and dreams. Because of her love for small businesses and leaders, Kim is a Certified Connexus Business Coach and is trained to equip and develop leaders who, in turn, develop leaders. She equips them to become financially free so they can fund their dreams and leave a legacy of impact and influence in life and business. Her passion is to see believers lead well and steward their gifts and finances for Kingdom work. Let her help you break your chains, give to what lights your fire, and create ripples of freedom that change lives far beyond your own.

www.kimsmithcoach.com

Chapter 10

Confidence Through Freedom

Danika Deva

So if the Son sets you free, you are truly free.
John 8:36 (NLT)

- Do you feel stuck in work and life?
- Do you want freedom but need help to get unstuck from yesterday's yuck?
- Do you want the confidence that can only come through true freedom in Christ?

We all want freedom from the past. Actually, we want it from the present and the future, too. Why? Because we know that freedom will allow us to be confident in life, through trials, and in our work and business.

Barriers to Freedom

The problem is, we get stuck. We carry baggage that doesn't serve us.

When we remove the baggage—the stuff holding us down, the luggage we carry—our training, experiences, and calling can take us on fulfilling adventures.

Let's look at some of the baggage we are carrying and why we need to let it go. Then we'll look at how we can convert that baggage into usable luggage through a Freedom Sweep.

Here are some common ways we often feel stuck. Do you resonate with any of them?

Are you...

- Stuck playing the replay button of hurtful words spoken over you?
- Angry at someone or something?
- Anxious or worried about life?
- Stuck in the cycle of striving and drivenness?
- So busy you can't breathe?
- Working in overdrive?
- Fearful of the future?
- Sick and tired of trying to do it all?
- Spinning in the addiction cycle and can't get out?
- Hating yourself or others?
- Feeling like you don't measure up or that you messed up too much?
- Living in regret?
- Discontent or depressed with your life and ready to escape?
- Too tired to be motivated?
- _____

If so, you are not alone. With a Freedom Sweep, you can get unstuck with a Biblically-based 5-step process. It is easy to learn and there is nothing to fear, because freedom is right around the corner.

Our confidence gets stuck when we are stuck.

We all get stuck at times, but we can't get *unstuck* if we don't know what to do. In my case, no one taught me how to get unstuck.

There was never a time when someone handed me a process to help me forgive seventy times seven or get rid of anxiety. I needed a tool, a process that I could use over and over, even though I wanted to get and stay free.

Psalm 51:10 (NIV) says, *Create in me a clean heart, O God, and renew a right spirit within me.* Oh how good it feels to be free. Are you ready to learn more?

Freedom at Last

A few years ago, two business associates called me to pray. I thought we were going to pray together, but instead, they wanted to pray for and with me. It was beautiful. As we prayed together, God showed me that I had bitterness towards some family members that I didn't know I held, even though I had forgiven them previously.

As I went before the Lord with the pain and wounds of their betrayal and repented of my bitterness, I was free at last.

After that prayer time together, I realized there may have been other areas where I was stuck and didn't know it. I asked the Lord to show me and found that I had fear and anxiety. Ironically, none of my friends would have said that I had either.

As I took fear and anxiety to the Lord, more freedom came. I sat before Him and asked if there were still other areas. Sure enough, there were several. I had a broken spirit from people who had greatly wounded me over the years. I had grief to give the Lord, and I harbored resentment.

I wondered how a Jesus girl had so much *yuck* to get rid of without even knowing it. Well, the answer is that we all have wounds, we all get stuck, and we all need a process to help us move forward. Sometimes we even need help from others as they pray with and guide us while we work through some of the stuff that has come our way.

As I worked through these areas of stuckness, God didn't just give me freedom—He gave me the tool to help others. He revealed the verses that went with each step, and I named the program **Freedom Sweep**. Out of my own freedom came my calling and passion: to help others get free and *stay* free.

After about 25 of my own Freedom Sweeps, my friend asked for one. And that is where Operation Freedom Sweep started.

Since then, I have walked friends, family members, worship leaders, pastors, missionaries, and many strangers through the process, providing them with an effective tool to use over and over.

Look what one woman said after her Freedom Sweep:

> I'm not the woman I always imagined I'd be. For the first time I can say it without shame. Without judgment. Immediately after my first Freedom Sweep, I felt lighter, like a heavy ickiness I didn't know I'd been carrying just evaporated. I'm learning to love who I am in Christ, so I'm better able to reach out in love to others without fear, and it's causing a ripple effect in my home. My heart, my mind, my soul, and my marriage felt like they were locked in molasses for years, that is, until I gave it all to Jesus during my Freedom Sweep. –Valerie

Other individuals going through a freedom sweep share how freeing it is, how great it is to have a tool to use when difficulties come their way, and that they want to use it to clear away more yuck.

The best part about a Freedom Sweep is that we can use it anytime and anyplace. Even as I write this, I had to stop and do a mini Freedom Sweep when I got frustrated with someone. Instead of getting mad and crying, stonewalling, blame-shifting, and all the other stuff we do, I just took it through the Freedom Sweep process. Boom! It's over. And believe me, it is so freeing not to keep the yuck with me.

By getting alone (or with a trained Freedom Sweep guide) and sitting before God asking Him for freedom and guidance, and then following the five Freedom Sweep steps, we can walk in a lifestyle of freedom. As we let the Spirit lead us through each step, He will reveal what we need to sweep up.

Freedom is FREE!

Freedom is free! Jesus died on the cross for our sins and because of that, we can give Him our sins, wounds, and problems. Yes, even the BIG ones!

By using a fill-in-the blank process, we can easily replace our yuck with peace, truth, trust, grace, love, and mercy.

In Ephesians 4:22-24 (NLT), we are told to *Throw off your old sinful nature and your former way of life, which is corrupted by lust and deception. Instead, let the Spirit renew your thoughts and attitudes. Put on your new nature, created to be like God—truly righteous and holy.*

We can do that because of what the Father has done for us. We can go to the Father again and again to guide us as we forgive others and repent before Him. Just like showering daily can keep us clean, cleaning our hearts is a necessity as well. Going to God in surrender and forgiveness regularly keeps us unstuck.

Freedom is a Lifestyle

Just so you know—a freedom lifestyle is ongoing. We must walk it out. Sometimes we need a Deep Clean, a Freedom Sweep, or a 10-Second Tidy. They all help us live in freedom.

As you walk away in freedom, know that the enemy will want to take you captive again. Remember, according to John 10:10 (NLT), *The thief's purpose is to steal and kill and destroy. My purpose is to give them a rich and satisfying life.* Freedom is a lifestyle!

A freedom lifestyle is ongoing. You must walk it out. As you walk in freedom, know that the enemy will want to take you captive again and again, but God's purpose is to give you a rich and satisfying life.

To walk in abundant life, you MUST believe that you have been freed from this issue and walk in faith, not fear. You must continue to fill your heart with God's Word to build your relationship with

God. The goal for a freedom sweep is this…**to know Christ in our minds and hearts and to experience Him as we walk in freedom**.

The Results of Freedom

Let's look at Ephesians 3:17-19 NLT:

And I pray that Christ will be more and more at home in your hearts, living within you as you trust in him. May your roots go down deep into the soil of God's marvelous love; and may you be able to feel and understand, as all God's children should, how long, how wide, how deep, and how high his love really is; and to experience this love for yourselves, though it is so great that you will never see the end of it or fully know or understand it. And so at last you will be filled up with God himself.

Some of the fabulous results of freedom are:

- Having trust and confidence in the Lord.
- Establishing roots that go deep down into the soil of God's marvelous love.
- Feeling and understanding how long, how wide, how deep, and how high His love really is.
- Experiencing Christ's love for yourselves.
- Being filled up with God Himself.

These are some amazing benefits of truly trusting Him. And with this surrender and trust, you can be truly free and live abundantly.

Just know that you are not alone. We are all working on this. As we walk the trust journey with Jesus and use this process to continually walk in freedom, we can confidently do what God has called us to do.

So if the Son sets you free, you are truly free.

John 8:36 (NLT)

* *If you need help with freedom and want more information about a Freedom Sweep, contact Danika Deva at* danikadeva.com

Chapter 11

Prosperity Part 1:
Cultivating Confidence in God's Plan for Your Prosperity:
Experiencing True Prosperity in the Seven Dimensions of Health

Ellen Boyer

Dear friend, I am praying that everything prosper with you and that you be in good health, as I know you are prospering spiritually.

3 John 1:2

- Did you know there is a difference between belief, trust, and confidence?
- Are you ready to break through the religious routine in your life?
- Do you know why all the other dimensions of health hinge on the Spiritual Dimension?

Unless otherwise noted, all scriptures are taken from the Complete Jewish Bible, CJB.

Cultivating Confidence

As we begin this adventure of confidence in God's plan for true prosperity in the seven dimensions of health, I must ask: What qualifications are needed for this task? What makes a difference in your confidence in God's plan for your prosperity? What specific preparation might make it possible to touch your heart in a way that will awaken a new understanding of that plan?

Core Values Dictate Your Response

We can only do what we believe God has created us to do. In my case, a close look at my core values has reinforced what I have known about myself for nearly 40 years. I am happiest, most ful-filled, and effective when I live my core values of **Influencing** others, causing them to **Awaken** to new possibilities, **Enlightening** them about a subject or situation, and **Teaching** and **Encouraging** them to experience all that God has provided.

How you respond depends on what your core values are. Whether you are aware of your core values is not at issue. We all have them, even if we haven't identified them or know how to discuss them.

Those values determine your response to this chapter. Your con-fidence in God's plan for your prosperity, expressed in the seven dimensions of health, will be effective only to the degree in which your values cause you to be receptive or not. It is my desire that you leave this experience enriched and with a changed life.

Your total health (true prosperity) depends on your core values and how you live true to them.

Why bring up motivating core values when we could leave that whole concept out and move on to the subject of God's plan for your prosperity? Because, like the phrase "the seven dimensions of health," the consideration of "core values" is a handy way to discuss a big subject. Your total health (true prosperity) depends on your core values and how you live true to them.

Core values are developed and can be positive or negative, de-pending on your life experiences. As God's Word works through the power of the Holy Spirit, you can—and will, change. The result is central to true prosperity—it dictates your health in all seven dimensions. Hopefully, some of you will change your mind about prosperity. Others will wake up to the possibility of experiencing confidence in God's plan. For a few, the light will come on that God *has* a plan for prosperity. Finally, I may be able to teach some of what the Bible says about that plan. I pray that you all will be encouraged to believe in God's plan for your prosperity with confidence.

What is Confidence in God's Plan?

How will we measure our confidence level if we don't clearly understand it? What *is* confidence in God's plan for true prosperity in the seven dimensions of health?

Modern dictionary definitions of the word *confidence* offer clues to the real meaning of the word as we use it here: The Merriam-Webster dictionary describes confidence as faith or belief that one will act correctly, properly, or effectively. We use that definition to express God's reliability in carrying out His plan for our prosperity. But, is believing that God is able and having faith in His good intentions the same as confidence?

Acknowledging what we understand to be God's attributes
and having confidence in those qualities
can be two different things.

We believe God is able. We have faith in His good intentions, but is that the same as confidence? Technically, yes. However, acknowledging what we understand to be God's attributes and having *confidence* in those qualities can be two different things.

Look at scripture and the original Hebrew and Greek texts concerning confidence. We find the concept of confidence is associated with "trust" and "hope," basically the same idea expressed in our modern dictionaries. The problem here is the difference in understanding what we have been taught about God's reliability to provide and the assurance that comes from the combined force of a spiritual experience that directs intellectual awareness and psychological development.

I realize that is a mouthful and takes us beyond this simple introduction to cultivating confidence. So, let's try to simplify it: It is one thing to know something and another to rely on it. Sometimes, we confuse knowing or familiarity with belief. Belief in a concept does not necessarily supply the confidence needed to act upon that belief.

Consider the small child who believes his father will catch him if he jumps off the side of the swimming pool into his arms. That child has not had enough negative life experiences to doubt his father. His brain is wired for optimism naturally[1] and he thinks he can trust his father. So, he jumps. Over time, he may have life experiences that modify his confidence in his father's reliability. Or, as he ages, encounters negative experiences, and loses trust in others, he may not be as willing to jump on command.

When we have negative experiences, they are so out of place in our naturally optimistic brain they get our attention, and we tend to focus on them. The negative affects us more because it is so unusual. The more negative experiences we encounter, the more we focus on them until our confidence weakens. Although we still believe we should trust, we are no longer confident enough to jump. Let's not spend too much time on this phenomenon, but know the result can affect our mental and physical health.

WAKE UP from Routine Religious Experiences

Our routinely religious experience as Christians contributes to a lack of confidence in God's Word. My combined core values compel me to be a disruptive force in the "normal" flow of traditional thinking. I intend to "shake the tree" of lackadaisical Bible reading patterns by encouraging you to hear what the Holy Spirit says about God's Word, not just what you've listened to since storytime in Sunday School.

For many of us, Bible stories are like our other childhood favorites—Little Red Riding Hood, The Three Little Pigs, or my favorite, Uncle Wiggly. You may be a lot younger than I am, so your list may be entirely different than mine. It doesn't matter what our personal favorites are. We never tire of hearing those stories and continue the tradition by reading them to our children and grandchildren. They are dependable, and they never change. We don't question the plot, and—the part that most concerns me—we don't believe them. There's no need to let them keep us awake, dreading the return of the big bad wolf (or whoever or whatever threatens the happy ending). It's only a story.

We should have the same concerns about our Bible reading habits. Even the good practices of routinely reading through the Bible every year or following a specific pattern of daily devotions or annual cycles of Bible reading, may lull us to sleep like bedtime stories. Yet, we never tire of hearing the story. It is dependable and never changes. We don't question the plot—but we don't *believe it*.

Even Good Ground Needs to be Cultivated.

I can almost hear you gasp at that statement, but if it is not valid, why do we find it necessary to cultivate our confidence in God's plan for our lives? As a disruptive force in religious "business as usual," I encourage you to look at the word "cultivate." Again, looking at Merriam-Webster, we see one definition of *cultivate* is to improve by labor, care, or study. In another sense, the word can describe the action of preparing the ground to be used for raising or fostering the growth of crops.

In scripture, we first see the use of the word "cultivate" in the second chapter of Genesis. But before you read on, I must warn you of yet another disruption of your routine Bible reading: I almost always quote from one of the Messianic Jewish translations.

I do this for two reasons. One is because the wording is unfamiliar. It makes us stop and read a passage we may have read repeatedly but never stopped to think about what it says. And two, I believe we cannot fully understand the ministry of Jesus on earth or His death on the cross unless we understand His Jewish heritage. Reading scripture as the Messianic Jewish believer reads it at least gives us pause:[2]

*Here is the history of the heavens and the earth when they were
created. On the day when ADONAI, God, made earth and heaven,
there was as yet no wild bush on the earth, and no wild plant
had as yet sprung up; for ADONAI, God, had not caused it to rain
on the earth, and there was no one to cultivate the ground.
Rather, a mist went up from the earth which watered the entire surface
of the ground. Then ADONAI, God, formed a person [Hebrew: adam]
from the dust of the ground [Hebrew: adamah] and breathed into his
nostrils the breath of Life, so that he became a living being.
ADONAI, God, planted a garden toward the east, in Eden,
and there he put the person whom he had formed.*

Genesis 2:4-8

Cultivation is a Requirement—not an option.

Notice that in this history of the heavens and the earth, because
there had been no rain, there was no wild bush or plant and, even
more interesting, no one to cultivate the ground. Cultivation is a requirement—not an option. As if in response to this deficiency, God
created a person, Adam, planted a garden east of Eden, and put
the man there.

It appears that even good ground benefits from cultivation. Can you
think of any garden with better, more productive soil than the Garden of Eden? God planted it east of Eden, and as far as we can tell
from the very first creative words God uttered when He said, "Let
there be light," everything He created was good. Yet that Garden
needed to be cared for and cultivated.

The bottom line is this: if we are to experience true prosperity as
God intended, even good ground needs cultivation. **Our confidence in Him and His provision for us increases with care and
cultivation.** His plan is in place, but if we are to experience it, we
must develop a new way of thinking about what has become familiar to us. We cannot continue to nod, say amen, and remain the
same.

As we choose to experience God's plan for true prosperity, we
will wake up to new possibilities in those old familiar stories we've

heard repeatedly. The light will come on in the true sense of the Word—by allowing Jesus, the Light of the World, to influence our thinking and change our minds. We will learn from the Teacher, not by reading words in a book called the Bible, but by the power of the Holy Spirit, who guides us into all truth. We will encourage one another as we become confident enough in God's plan for true prosperity in the seven dimensions of health that we jump into the Father's outstretched arms.

Why Seven Dimensions of Health?

If you search the internet (or library references—I give the nod here to those among us who love to hold books in their hands) for "seven dimensions of health," you will find article after article on the subject. Almost all those articles agree on the basic concept of seven dimensions of health; only the descriptions and treatment of each vary.

The concept of seven dimensions of health began in 1976 when Dr. Bill Hettler, co-founder of the National Wellness Institute, defined six dimensions of wellness: Physical, Emotional, Intellectual, Spiritual, Social, and Occupational. He "created this six-dimension model to teach the public about the interconnectedness of each dimension and how all these factors add up to create a holistic sense of wellness and fulfillment. The list has since expanded to include a seventh dimension, Environmental wellness." [3]

I have adopted the idea that health involves more than the human body and emotions. As I realized that health is more than how much weight I need to lose to be healthy, I stumbled upon two sources that have transformed my understanding of myself in ways I could never have imagined. These two sources have contributed to my decisions, commitment, and knowledge of the interaction of the seven dimensions of health.

The foundation for this awareness was laid in 2019 when I discovered Jim Lupkin and his book *Never Run Out of People to Talk to: Social Media for your Business Success* [4] and, a little later, the updated edition, *Predictive Social Media: A Guide to Mastering Core*

Values, Relationships, and a Disruptive System That Is Changing the World of Business.[5]

Jim's focus on understanding core values in creating authentic relationships and growing your business changed my thinking about what makes me who I am and set me on a path that has brought me here today. In the process, I joined Jim and his team as he launched a new company focusing on the seven dimensions of health.

As a result of what I learned in the process of certification in Jim's Predictive Social Media system, I became friends on social media with Karen Lindwall-Bourg. So, providentially, I stumbled upon her book *Wellness: The Awareness of the Whole Individual.*[6] Karen and her collaborators authored this book from the perspective of professional counselors. They use the concept of attending to all dimensions of wellness when listening to and guiding their clients. I use the word *stumbled* as I smile, remembering how blown away I was when I realized the path God had taken me down to get me to where He wanted me: *With your ears you will hear a word from behind you: This is the way; stay on it, whether you go to the right or the left* (Isaiah 30:21). The result of those two encounters is what you are reading here—and all that will come after it!

God's Plan for True Prosperity in Scripture

Discovering a concept in a book floating around the internet is one thing. Confirming the idea in scripture and assessing it to determine if it is *God-breathed and is valuable for teaching the truth, convicting of sin, correcting faults and training in right living* (2 Timothy 3:16), is quite another. I was excited about Jim's and Karen's introduction to the concept of the seven dimensions of health and was compelled to find out if scripture supported it.

As is my practice, I began my search for scriptural confirmation "in the beginning"—Genesis, Chapter 1. My philosophy that all scripturally sound teaching can find support in the first five books of the Bible has stood me in good stead for well over 40 years. If I could find confirmation that God provided seven dimensions of health for Adam and Eve, then I could go with it!

Like our first introduction to any new idea, entity, or individual, the initial exposure to scripture does not necessarily tell the whole story. I have read or heard the opening chapters in the Old Testament all my life, but my understanding of God's plan for man's prosperity began when I studied a single verse in the New Testament. I quote it here from, guess what, the Complete Jewish Translation:

Dear friend, I am praying that everything prosper with you and that you be in good health, as I know you are prospering spiritually.

3 John 1:2

In the King James Version of the Bible, it is not so clear that John is speaking of prosperity in a broader sense than the primary Merriam-Webster definition of "to succeed in an enterprise or activity, *especially to achieve economic success*."

Everything Hinges on Prospering Spiritually

The secondary definition—to become strong and flourishing—is closer to what I believe John's intent is in this verse: that Gaius prosper in both his physical and spiritual health:

Beloved, I wish above all things that thou mayest prosper and be in health,even as thy soul prospereth.

3 John 1:2 (KJV)

Unfortunately, the King James Version of this scripture is one of the primary texts some believers use to support what is known as the "prosperity gospel." I agree that God's will and plan for humanity are financial and physical health, as expressed in this verse. However, as is often the case, it is taken out of context in the prosperity gospel:

A theology of a Protestant subculture largely occupied by (but not limited to) Pentecostal and charismatic believers that posits financial blessings and physical health are God's will for the faithful—is an especially pernicious plague in the world, now fully exported and a global affront to true Christianity. And its problems aren't merely theological. The prosperity gospel movement exploits the poor and many others in ways implicit and explicit that often cross fully into the category of spiritual abuse.[7]

For many, confidence in God's plan for true prosperity was lost, not cultivated, due to this teaching.

This example of confidence lost is not unique. If we look at traditional Christian teaching, we can find many examples of theologies built on a single, well-known Bible verse. Jesus understood this tendency and addressed it directly when He confronted the Pharisees. They accepted the written Word as inspired by God but gave equal authority to oral tradition, saying their practices went back to Moses. Unfortunately, as the Pharisaic rules evolved over the centuries, and the "Thou shalts" and "Thou shalt nots" increased, they continued to add to God's Word, which is forbidden in Deuteronomy 4:2:

In order to obey the mitzvot of ADONAI your God which I am giving you, do not add to what I am saying, and do not subtract from it.

Deuteronomy 4:2

I call God's plan for prosperity "true prosperity" to indicate I have taken a step away from the "prosperity gospel" and the burden of the law Jesus came to overcome (Galatians 5:1 KJV). My objective is to focus on Genesis 1:2. Here, we see the "*earth was unformed and void, darkness was on the face of the deep, and the Spirit of God hovered over the surface of the water.*" That action of the Holy Spirit prepared the way for the creative power of God, the Father (YAHWEH), to speak His plan into existence. As a result, Jesus, the Light of the World, sprang out of the east (Luke 1:78 KJV), and God began preparing a place for humankind on earth, as it is in heaven (Matthew 6:9-13).

Adopting the seven dimensions of health improved my understanding and communication of true prosperity. I use that concept to manage chunks of information—not to develop a new theology— the study of religious faith, practice, and experience.[8]

As I mentioned earlier, the concept of the seven dimensions of health is not new. It has been around since the 1970s and is used by healthcare organizations, providers, counselors, and coaches to help "people become aware of and make choices toward a more successful existence."[9]

Spiritual Health is Foundational

In its most basic structure, the seven dimensions of health inform and encourage us to proactively attend to each of the following human systems: physical, emotional, intellectual, spiritual, social, occupational, and environmental. I have renamed the "emotional" dimension "psychological" and rearranged the order in which they appear in my discussion and illustrations to reflect their dependency on each other more accurately.

Spiritual health is foundational to every other dimension of health.

For my purposes, the names and order of the seven dimensions of health are as follows:

- Spiritual Health
- Intellectual Health
- Psychological Health
- Physical Health
- Social Health
- Occupational Health
- Environmental Health

I list Spiritual Health first because it is foundational to every other dimension of health.

Unless our Spiritual Health is firmly grounded in a relationship of confidence in God's plan for true prosperity, we cannot be healthy in the other six dimensions. I base this belief on 3 John 1:2, where John's prayer that "you be in health" is followed by his declaration that he knows his friend Gaius is "prospering spiritually." Additionally, Romans 8:9-11, and other verses, remind us that the Holy Spirit unites with the human spirit and works to perfect every area of our lives:

> *But you, you do not identify with your old nature but with the Spirit—*
> *provided the Spirit of God is living inside you, for anyone*
> *who doesn't have the Spirit of the Messiah doesn't belong to him.*
> *However, if the Messiah is in you, then, on the one hand, the body is dead*
> *because of sin; but, on the other hand, the Spirit is giving Life*
> *because God considers you righteous. And if the Spirit of the*
> *One who raised Yeshua from the dead is living in you, then the*
> *One who raised the Messiah Yeshua from the dead will also give*
> *Life to your mortal bodies through his Spirit living in you.*

Romans 8:9-11

With spiritual health as our foundation, we have assurance our "temple" will be whole:

> *Don't you know that you people are God's temple and that*
> *God's Spirit lives in you? So if anyone destroys God's temple,*
> *God will destroy him. For God's temple is holy,*
> *and you yourselves are that temple.*

1 Corinthians 3:16, 17

If we listen and respond to the thou shalts
we do not need the thou shalt nots.

Typically, the only time we hear about our bodies being God's temple is when we are warned what not to put in it or do to it, correct? Surely you've listened to those sermons and all the other "thou shalt not" messages we, as Christians, hear. Yes, I acknowledge that the truth of our righteousness through Christ Jesus is preached and taught in our Bible Schools and studies, but when it comes to our physical habits, we hear the negative *do not* more often than the positive *do*. If we listen and respond to the "thou shalts" we do not need the "thou shalt nots."

I referred to Dr. Caroline Leaf's research on the brain's naturally positive state earlier when talking about the confidence a small child has when she jumps from the side of the swimming pool into

103

her father's outstretched arms.[10] As I understand Dr. Leaf's assertion that the brain is naturally "wired" for optimism, "thou shalt not" does not positively influence our behavior. We can confirm the validity of that notion by looking at the results Moses had when he went up to Mount Sinai and returned to present what we know as the Ten Commandments to Israel.

The Israelites ramped up their misdeeds in Moses' absence and built a golden calf to worship. When Moses returned from the presence of God with the two tablets on which were written the Ten Commandments, he saw what God had already told him had taken place (Exodus 32:1-4):

> When the people saw that Moshe was taking a long time to come down from the mountain, they gathered around Aharon and said to him, "Get busy; and make us gods to go ahead of us; because this Moshe, the man that brought us up from the land of Egypt — we don't know what has become of him." Aharon said to them, "Have your wives, sons and daughters strip off their gold earrings; and bring them to me." The people stripped off their gold earrings and brought them to Aharon. He received what they gave him, melted it down, and made it into the shape of a calf.

In his anger at seeing the people not only worshiping the substitute god they had made but dancing in celebration at what they had created for themselves, Moses angrily broke the tablets—as if to demonstrate to the Israelites what they had done. Before he had even presented the tablets of law designed to govern their behavior, the Israelites had broken the first four commandments. We'll come back to that shortly.

The point here is that the Sunday School version of Moses and the Ten Commandments is simple, much-loved, incomplete, and much more complicated. It portrays God's provision for His chosen people, Israel—and you and me. Unfortunately, as Gentile believers, we get only one tiny negative glimpse of the picture. As a result, we learn to follow a Gentile Jesus and live by a list of rules that do little to promote our understanding of God's plan for true prosperity.

There is neither time nor space in this writing to tell the whole story, so accept the challenge and read it for yourselves. According to

Hebrew scholars and the Old Testament translations Christians depend on, Moses made eight trips up and down that mountain. The children of Israel, under Moses' leadership, had an encounter with God and heard His voice before Moses made his first trip up Mount Sinai. God's power and glory were too much for them to handle, so they sent Moses to meet God on the mountaintop; they agreed to obey whatever He told Moses they should do. Moses returned with the Ten Commandments—and told the people what God had instructed them. They agreed to obey once again. Moses returned to the mountaintop, and 40 days later reappeared with the stone tablets he later broke. Then Moses returned to God's presence, and after another 40 days, descended the mountain again with the second set of tablets—and the story goes on…[11]

Are You AWAKE Yet?

Has your thinking been challenged? Have you been awakened? Are you ready to change your patterns from religious routine?

One way to begin is by rereading and rethinking the story of the Ten Commandments. It is an excellent place to start.

Remember, before Moses had even presented the tablets of law designed to govern their behavior, the Israelites had broken the first four commandments. They didn't even have the excuse that they "didn't know what the law was" because they had heard it with their own ears and agreed to obey before Moses ever brought the tablets down from the mountain. But how is it they broke the *first four commandments*?

Have you ever wondered why, when Jesus was confronted by a Pharisee lawyer who was hoping to tempt Him by asking which was the greatest commandment, Jesus summed up the whole law into two commandments? Even though the Pharisee knew all about the Ten Commandments, Jesus told him, *You are to love ADONAI your God with all your heart and with all your soul and with all your strength. This is the greatest and most important mitzvah. And a second is similar to it, You are to love your neighbor as yourself. All of the Torah and the Prophets are dependent on these two mitzvot* (Matthew 22:26-40).

Or, in the New King James Version, *You shall love the LORD your God with all your heart, with all your soul, and with all your mind.*

This is the first and great commandment. And the second is like it: You shall love your neighbor as yourself. On these two commandments hang all the Law and the Prophets (Matthew 22:36-40).

A second look at the Ten Commandments makes Jesus' summary of the law clear: the first four commandments focus on our love for God:

1. You are to have no other gods before me,

2. You are not to make idols and bow down before them,

3. You are not to use the name of God in vain or lightly, and

4. Remember the Sabbath and keep it holy.

The last six commandments focus on our love for our fellow man.[12] Loving God comes first and makes it possible to love others. When the Israelites broke the first four commandments while Moses was with God, they made it impossible to obey the remaining six. The whole law was broken, as Moses demonstrated when he broke both tablets.

On Moses' return to the mountain, he offered himself in atonement for their sin, just as Jesus has done for us. That is the good, positive news our brains are wired to hear. None other will produce God's plan for true prosperity and health in every human system. The *Thou shalt not* approach to health is counterproductive.

Jesus, our Savior, has seen our condition and pleaded with the Father to spare us the results of our idolatry. He has atoned for our sin by His death on the cross and presented His blood to the Father so that we might have life more abundantly. That life includes perfect health—true prosperity. He has sent the Holy Spirit to bring to our remembrance everything He has done and said on our behalf, including His words that very clearly emphasize the power of the positive statements He made about the commandments.

Instead of ten commandments, we have one: eat the fruit from the Tree of Life. Our spiritual health springs forth in our obedience to this, the first commandment in the Garden of Eden:

*In the beginning was the Word, and the Word was with God,
and the Word was God. He was with God in the beginning.
All things came to be through him, and without him nothing made had
being. In him was life, and the life was the light of mankind.
The light shines in the darkness, and the darkness has not suppressed it.*

John 1:1-5

With spiritual health as our foundation, we can be healthy in every other dimension. We experience God's plan when we experience intellectual, psychological, physical, occupational, and environmental health because we are whole spiritually. Only then can we love our neighbor as ourselves. That is God's plan for true prosperity in the seven dimensions of health.

In this, we can have confidence.

Endnotes

1. Leaf, Caroline Dr. 2020. "Can You Train Yourself to Become a More Optimistic Person?" 12 15. Accessed 8 10, 2022. https://drleaf.com/blogs/news/can-you-make-yourself-a-more-optimistic-person

2. When you don't understand what you are reading, stop and look that passage of scripture up; read it in your favorite translation or try a new version—anything to stimulate your interest and understanding.

3. The Blog: *The 7 Dimensions of Wellness, Explained* Accessed 8 10, 2022. https://blog.alomoves.com/lifestyle/the-7-dimensions-of-wellness-explained

4. Lupkin, Jim. 2020. Never run Out of People to Talk to: Social Media for your Business Success. Kindle Edition. Kindle Edition. https://www.amazon.com/Never-Run-Out-People-Talk-ebook/

5. Lupkin, Jim. 2021. Predictive Social Media: A Guide to Mastering Core Values, Relationships, and a Disruptive System That Is Changing the World of Business. Kindle Edition. SPOV Publishing.

6. Lindwall-Bourg, Karen. 2016. Wellness: The Awareness of the Whole Individual. 1st. RHEMA Publishing House. Accessed 8 10, 2022

7. In Our Rejection of the Prosperity Gospel, Are We Missing God's Provision? https://www.christianitytoday.com/pastors/2021/fall/rejection-prosperity-gospel-missing-gods-provision.html

8. Merriam-Webster Online Dictionary copyright © 2012 by Merriam-Webster, Incorporated

9. Hettler, Bill, MD. Origin of the Hettler Model of Wellness: Balance the Six Dimensions of your life. https://www.hettler.com/

10. Leaf, Caroline Dr. 2020. *Can You Train Yourself to Become a More Optimistic Person?* 12 15. Accessed 8 10, 2022. https://drleaf.com/blogs/news/can-you-make-yourself-a-more-optimistic-person

11. Schwartz, B.J. 2013. What Really Happened at Mount Sinai? Accessed 8 10, 2022. https://www.thetorah.com/article/what-really-happened-at-mount-sinai

12. Foundations for Living: *The Ten Commandments: Loving God: The First Four Commandments.* Accessed 8 10, 2022. https://harvest.org/know-god-article/loving-god-the-first-four-commandments/

Definitions throughout the chapter: Merriam-Webster Online Dictionary copyright © 2022 by Merriam-Webster, Incorporated https://www.merriam-webster.com/dictionary/

Chapter 12

Prosperity Part 2:
Cultivating Confidence in God's Plan for Your Prosperity:
Experiencing True Prosperity in the Seven Dimensions of Health
Ellen Boyer

Unless otherwise noted, all scriptures are taken from the Complete Jewish Bible, CJB.

Why Seven Dimensions of Health?

Having established my process and purpose in adopting the concept of seven dimensions of health when looking at God's plan for true prosperity, you might find it interesting that we end up with the number seven. Bill Hettler's original six dimensions of health[1] are noteworthy; after all, the number six corresponds with God creating man on the sixth day, and we are talking about human health here. With the addition of environmental health, we now have a total of seven aspects of health to consider. Well, that makes sense, too. God's work was finished on the sixth day, but He did not go about His business and move on to another task of being God the next day. On the seventh day, God rested—and He has commanded us to rest and keep the seventh day holy.

One of the unique features of the seventh day in the creation story is the absence of a beginning and end. On each of the six days recorded in Genesis 1, there is morning and evening, a first, second, third, fourth, fifth, and sixth day. However, the seventh day is not described as having morning and evening; instead, it is meant to be separate and holy.

> *Thus the heavens and the earth were finished,*
> *along with everything in them. On the seventh day God was finished*
> *with his work which he had made, so he rested on the seventh day*
> *from all his work which he had made. God blessed the seventh day and*
> *separated it as holy; because on that day God rested from all his work*
> *which he had created, so that it itself could produce.*
> Genesis 2:1-3

God not only created the earth to be inhabited by humans; His intention is that man be in complete control of that world. In His rest, He has taken His hands off and given us free reign to care for and rule over our legacy. Adam and Eve had detailed instructions from God that guaranteed their success—if only they had followed them.

To assist us in our recovery from our ancestor's errors, God has provided a seasoned Tutor, the Holy Spirit. In addition, God knows our inherited tendencies toward disobedience and has provided an Advocate—one who pleads the cause of another—who has paid our fines in advance. His name is Jesus. We also have a very detailed handbook, the Bible. It contains our history, instructions for the present generation to follow, and a description of the reward that awaits us when we do so.

In the history section of our handbook, we read the rules God gave our earliest ancestors when it became apparent they needed a little help if they were going to live long enough to enjoy their inheritance. The shortened version is known as the Ten Commandments. In their simplest form, the first four commandments are:

1. You are to have no other gods before me.
2. You are not to make idols and bow down before them.
3. You are not to use the name of God in vain or lightly.
4. Remember the Sabbath and keep it holy.

These first four commandments point to God and our relationship with Him, or, as Jesus summed them up, *You are to love ADONAI your God with all your heart and with all your soul and with all your strength. This is the greatest and most important mitzvah* (Matthew 22:37).

In loving God with all your heart, soul, and strength, you are engaging all of you, as you are represented in the seven dimensions of health, with Him—and resting. Remembering the Sabbath and keeping it holy is God's plan for true prosperity in a nutshell. That holiness is found in our confidence that God has made every provision for our well-being. As believers, fully confident of that plan, we rest in His design for our wholeness—separated and holy.

> The adjective *holy* comes from the Old English word *hālig* and is related to the German word *heilig*, meaning blessed. There is a relationship between *holy* and *whole*, and the religious sense probably developed from keeping believers spiritually whole— and pure. A place, object, or person who has been blessed can be described as holy, meaning "associated with God."[2]

God's plan for true prosperity is that in keeping the Sabbath, we are holy, as He is holy. Do you believe God has ever been less than whole? Has He ever been less than holy? If we, being made in His image, are less than either—whole or holy—we are not expressions of His plan. We are ignorant because we have been deceived, just as Eve was deceived in the Garden of Eden.

As people who obey God, do not let yourselves be shaped by the evil desires you used to have when you were still ignorant. On the contrary, following the Holy One who called you, become holy yourselves in your entire way of life; since the Tanakh says, "You are to be holy because I am holy."

1 Peter 1:14-16

Now, let's return to the number seven and the dimensions of health. Glen Carpenter's book, *God's Numbers - A Study Guide in Bible Symbolism*, portrays the number seven in scripture as used "extensively to denote a complete period, or full cycle. Hence, it represents completion, perfection, and fullness in terms of Divine workings. The full seven days of creation are a Divine work; in other words, the Sabbath was a cessation of work in creating material things, but the Sabbath represents an active rest." [3]

I love that description, *an active rest*; that sounds like confidence. Our seven dimensions of health represent completion, perfection, and fullness, all ours as we actively engage with our Maker under the direction of the Holy Spirit. We can have confidence that God works in us *"both to will and to do of His good pleasure."*

By now, you've got it: for our purpose, there are seven dimensions of health. Based on my understanding of God's plan for true prosperity, I have ordered them as follows:

1. Spiritual
2. Intellectual
3. Psychological
4. Physical
5. Social
6. Occupational
7. Environmental

The Seven Dimensions of Health Define Man

In deciding to order the seven dimensions of health as I have, I considered each dimension and how it relates to the others. For instance, what is spiritual health, and what has it to do with psychological or intellectual health? As you have already seen, it is my position that human health cannot be complete unless we are spiritually whole. So, which of the seven dimensions of health comes next? I realized that I would have to look at what the Bible says about the creation of man to find that answer.

If it is true that God created man in His image, it is only logical that man looks like God. Since we have no experience with God in a physical form, we depend on scripture to portray Him until we see "Him as He is" (1 John 3:2b). In the meantime, if we are to be like Him, we must look at His attributes and allow Him, by the power of the Holy Spirit, to shape us. To discover His characteristics, we again begin at the beginning.

In Genesis, we first see the Holy Spirit hovering over the dark, unformed, deep. Second, God (YAHWEH) speaks. And finally, the Son—the Light of the World—*is*. This description of God at work lays the groundwork for our understanding that God is a triune being. That is, He looks like three persons in one. The presence and action of a triune God are confirmed when we read Genesis 1:26-27:

Then God said, "Let us make humankind in our image, in the likeness of ourselves; and let them rule over the fish in the sea, the birds in the air, the animals, and over all the earth, and over every crawling creature that crawls on the earth." So God created humankind in his own image; in the image of God he created him: male and female he created them.

Note that God did not say, *I think I will make a man.* There is no question that He said, *Let us make a man.* God is three in one: God the Father, Son, and Holy Spirit. If we are in His image (made to "look" like Him), we are three persons in one. Of course, we are not gods; we are humans that reflect God's attributes. As triune beings, we emulate or match Him in our humanness. We can see that likeness in 1 Thessalonians 5:23-24:

May the God of Shalom make you completely holy—may your entire spirit, soul and body be kept blameless for the coming of our Lord Yeshua the Messiah. The one calling you is faithful, and He will do it.

God created a body without life when He molded man from the earth. It was not until He breathed into His nostrils that man became a body with a spirit that could communicate with God, also a spirit. That body and spirit were incomplete, not equipped to live in the natural world without becoming a living soul. The soul is the ingredient necessary for the spirit, in a physical body, to function in the environment God had created. Hebrews 4:12 says:

See, the Word of God is alive! It is at work and is sharper than any double-edged sword—it cuts right through to where soul meets spirit and joints meet marrow, and it is quick to judge the inner reflections and attitudes of the heart.

God made man in His image—completely holy—with the intention that we experience wholeness within His promise to faithfully bring it about.

The word *heart* is often substituted for the word *soul*. The Greek word translated as *soul* in Hebrews 4:12 is *kardia*. We get our English word *cardiac*, referring to the heart, from it. In our experience, the heart is the most crucial organ a human has. If it stops, we die. Reverse that train of thought, and you see that we are not alive until the heart starts, which explains the importance of man becoming a living soul.

The soul allows the body's brain to unravel all the signals sent to it. Consider how overwhelming that might be. Without a soul, those signals can't be sorted into organized information; and man is paralyzed, unable to function in his environment. There is no life in him—and no learning. Adam certainly would not have been capable of naming the animals. How would he know what it meant to cultivate that garden where God put him without a functioning soul? I can see him now, "Uh, huh? What'cha mean? Cultivate?"

I hope you are beginning to understand the crucial role of the soul. It is who you have become, the combination of your intellectual and psychological nature, that makes you the unique person you are. You become that person as your environment bombards you with signals to be filtered through your five physical senses, directed by your brain, and evaluated by your spirit. Adam, the original man, lived after God breathed the breath of life into his nostrils (his body), and Adam *became*. The Hebrew word translated *became* means "to be conspicuous among a number, to be eminent, distinguished by a thing"—that is, "to be becoming, seemly, fit."[4] Adam was distinguished by his nature. The triune God squeezed some earth (clay) to form his body, breathed His breath of Life into him, and he became a living soul.

Let's see if I can summarize that in a few easy-to-read sentences. God is a triune spiritual being, capable of expressing himself in physical form: God the Father (YAHWEH), God the Son (Jesus or Messiah), and God the Holy Spirit. Each person of the Godhead is unique but is inseparable from the other two. This triune God created humankind in His image—to "look" like Him—in a physical form, capable of expressing himself spiritually. We live in a body housing; we are a spirit able to communicate with our Maker while functioning in the physical realm with the benefit of a soul. Each of the seven dimensions of health can be associated with one or more of the three expressions of this triune God.

And now, we are ready to define, put into perspective, and consider the interaction of each of the seven dimensions of health.

The Seven Dimensions of Health—What are They and How Do They Interact

Spiritual Health

Definition of Spirit

An animating or vital principle held to give life to physical organisms; a supernatural being or essence: such as HOLY SPIRIT.

Perspective

From our perspective, we have already established that our spiritual condition is the foundation of God's plan for true prosperity. All the other dimensions of health are dependent on that infrastructure. To the extent we are unsure of who God is and what His plan for man entails, we are not well. If we understand who He is, as expressed in His description of Himself, we can confidently walk in His plan for man.

Application

We can describe spiritual health as *entering into God's rest*. Hebrews 4:1-3 underscores my earlier observation, that our confidence in His plan for true prosperity provides us Sabbath rest from work—from *doing*. It is His good pleasure to do it:

> *For God is the one working among you both the willing and the working for what pleases him.*

Philippians 2:13

Our spiritual health improves when we understand that when Jesus said, *It is finished* (John 19:30), His mission to redeem us from the works of the law—the Thou shalt nots—was complete. Galatians 2:16 tells us:

> *...even so, we have come to realize that a person is not declared righteous by God on the ground of his legalistic observance of Torah commands, but through the Messiah Yeshua's*

trusting faithfulness. Therefore, we too have put our trust in Messiah Yeshua and become faithful to him, so that we might be declared righteous on the ground of the Messiah's trusting faithfulness and not on the ground of our legalistic observance of Torah commands. For on the ground of legalistic observance of Torah commands, no one will be declared righteous.

No amount of doing the right thing or religiously keeping those ten commandments or any other ritual of religion will restore us to the condition of man in the Garden of Eden—pure and undefiled. But just as God provided a covering for Adam and Eve when they stood before Him, exposed and ashamed of their sin (Gen 3:21), the blood of Jesus covers the evidence of our sinful condition and restores us to our rightful place of what we call spiritual health. In Him, we can be as He is, at rest, daily living the Sabbath—as a day that has no beginning or end.

Intellectual Health

Definition of Intellect

The power of knowing is distinguished from the power to feel and to will: the capacity for knowledge; the capacity for rational or intelligent thought especially when highly developed.

Perspective

To limit this discussion, I will assume we can agree that a brain is needed to have the power of knowing, or intellect. I think we can also agree that a brain is not enough. When God finished creating the earth from which He fashioned Adam, He included a brain, but that doesn't seem enough to produce human intellect. It seems plausible that when God breathed the breath of life into his nostrils, the man started the process of becoming a living being (soul). Intellect, then, is a function of a human receiving input via a body part, the brain, and having the ability to do something with that information that contributes to his development or stimulates action.

I find it thought-provoking that the dictionary definition distinguishes intellect from some unspecified process known to have the power to feel and to will. This indicates that what you know must be processed in some other way than intellectually. From my perspective, that other way is via the psyche, or psychological health. Once again, we see that man mirrors God's triune image. Body, spirit, and soul are interdependent.

Application

God planted a garden toward the East in Eden and "caused to grow every tree pleasing in appearance and good for food, including the tree of life in the middle of the garden and the tree of the knowledge of good and evil (Genesis 2:8). Then He put the person He had created within it.

And this is where the interaction of the intellect and psyche (psychological health) comes in. In some mysterious way, God created man in His image, but with free will. Simply put, God handed over His authority to Adam with six specific instructions (Genesis 2 & 3). (I can't resist the urge to remind you that the number six is associated with man). God told him to:

1. be fruitful, multiply, and fill the earth,
2. subdue the earth,
3. rule over the fish in the sea, the birds in the air and every living creature that crawls on the earth,
4. cultivate and care for the garden,
5. eat from the Tree of Life in the middle of the garden, and
6. he was NOT to eat the fruit of the tree of the knowledge of good and evil.

Of course, Adam had the intellectual capability to understand and obey these instructions; otherwise, an all-knowing and all-wise God would not impose them. That fits our dictionary definition of intellect: the power of knowing. But, how does knowing get transferred into doing—the function of a physical body?

Before giving Adam the first of those six instructions, God provided everything necessary to be fruitful and multiply. He said, *It isn't good that the person should be alone. I will make for him a companion suitable for helping him* (Genesis 2:18). However, God did not immediately create Eve. First, He spoke the animals and birds into existence and gave Adam the responsibility of naming them. In

Hebrew, the word name indicates two things here: declaring sovereignty over the thing named and pronouncing the nature of that thing.

Now that's the intellect in action. None of the creatures Adam named were comparable to him, so God fashioned a woman as his companion. Adam could know each animal's characteristics and named them accordingly. But how did he know what his own needs were? How did he compare the nature of each bird and animal with his own and find them wanting? His intellect (just knowing) interacted with his spirit (in touch with God and His wisdom) and the next dimension of health on our list, his psyche, "*the psychological influences on a person's emotions and feelings*" (my italics).[5]

Psychological Health

Definition of Psychology
The mental or behavioral characteristics of an individual or group.

Perspective

Our dictionary definition of psychology hints at the impossibility of separating spiritual, intellectual, and psychological health into three neat little packages. Mental and behavioral characteristics are interdependent—they influence each other. The outcome depends on the influence of the spirit.

I have used the term "core values" to describe what develops from the interaction of intellect and psyche, as I define it here. Our core values are what make us who we are. If the life we have created for ourselves (or, to give you an out, we have been forced into) does not complement our core values, we cannot be at rest—the state of spiritual wellness. To put Adam's conclusion that none of the birds or animals God had created were compatible into modern-day terms, we could say that the animals and birds did not have the same core values he had. Some animals and birds are brilliant but lack the mental or behavioral characteristics humans have and are not a match.

In the case of Adam, newly inspired by the breath of God and not yet exposed to the negative effect of the serpent, the outcome was favorable. Adam recognized that the birds and animals were not created in the image of God like he was and could not satisfy his need for companionship (i.e. social health). So God made a woman from Adam's rib, an apt companion for the man from whom she came.

Application

Core values form over time as our spiritual, intellectual, psychological, physical, social, occupational, and environmental influences interact. Every natural and spiritual event challenges psychological development and health. Stronger or repetitive forces (either positive or negative) impact our value system most. If our environment is predominantly spiritually healthy, we stand a better chance of developing robust spiritual health. It follows that our intellectual and psychological health will be in tune with our spiritual health and with God.

Your total health depends on your core values and how you live true to them. Core values are developed and can be positive or negative, depending on your life experiences. As God's Word works through the power of the Holy Spirit, values can, and will, change. That change brings us closer to true prosperity. In their most straightforward form, we find a list of core values in Galatians 5:22-23:

> But the fruit of the Spirit is love, joy, peace, patience, kindness, goodness, faithfulness, humility, self control. Nothing in the Torah stands against such things.

Notice that these nine characteristics are the fruit of the Spirit. You may remember when God gave Adam authority over all He had created, the fifth instruction was to eat of the Tree of Life. How better to describe the fruit of that tree than "the fruit of the Spirit"?

Jesus, who came to restore us to life, has revealed Himself to us through the Spirit of truth, the Holy Spirit. To the degree that we allow Him to lead us into all truth, we will bear His fruit, which is love—a one-word description of the core value that best describes God, working in us both to will and do His good pleasure (Philippians 2:13, KJV). But what about those other values listed as the fruit of the Spirit—joy, peace, patience, kindness, goodness, faithfulness, humility, and self-control? Those are expressions of the nature of God, the thing that makes Him who He is: representations of His love.

Physical Health

Definition of Physical
*Having material existence: perceptible especially through the senses and subject to the laws of nature; of or relating to the body.**

Perspective

As I have ordered the seven dimensions of health, physical health is pivotal. It is at the mercy of our spiritual, intellectual, and psychological health in that it is impossible to be physically healthy unless those other areas of health are sound. Similarly, our social, occupational, and environmental health depend on how well we function physically.

The fact that Adam was created in the image of God dictated his health originally. He was whole and unable to die in that state. Had Adam and Eve eaten the fruit of the Tree of Life in the Garden, they would not have known death. Eating the fruit of the Tree of Knowledge of Good and Evil, a violation of the sixth and final instruction God gave in the beginning, ensured their demise: *You are not to eat from it, because on the day that you eat from it, it will become certain that you will die* (Genesis 2:16).

Some refute the accuracy of the Bible based on the fact that Adam and Eve did not fall over dead the minute they ate the fruit of that tree; however, they began the process of learning to die from that moment. And we have become experts at dying as a result. We call it aging and treat it as a natural process. Now we die more successfully than we live. Look at man's life span from the beginning of time until now to confirm that statement. Adam did eventually die, but he, and generations after him, lived almost 1000 years. "Today, man's maximum life span is about 120 years, and our average life expectancy is still only 70–80 years—just as it was when the 90th Psalm was written 3,400 years ago!" [6]

Application

Over the centuries since that day in a garden where man had absolute authority and freedom to control his destiny, but violated God's life preserving commandment, we have evolved. Unfortunately, our shortened life span indicates that our species' evolution has moved toward our demise rather than regaining our former state of health. Man's intellect has produced unimaginable "progress" in science to overcome the results of disobeying God's commandments. But our attempts to overcome death by our dependence on the knowledge of good and evil we gained without God's wisdom to guide us, will fail if we ignore the solution that has been there all along.

Death entered in because Adam did not obey a thou shalt not— God's commandment not to eat of the Tree of Good and Evil. We experience death because Adam did not obey a thou shalt—to eat of the Tree of Life. Had he been obedient, Adam would have understood God's instruction to be fruitful, multiply, fill the earth and subdue it, rule over the fish in the sea, the birds in the air and every living creature that crawls on the earth (Genesis 1:28). He would have used his authority to rule over that serpent when he came to tempt Eve.

Social Health

Definition of Social

Of or relating to human society, the interaction of the individual and the group, or the welfare of human beings as members of society.

Perspective

God understood the need for healthy social interaction: ADONAI, God, said, *It isn't good that the person should be alone. I will make for him a companion suitable for helping him* (Genesis 2:16). In His love, mercy, and understanding that Adam could not fulfill His instructions to be fruitful, multiply, fill the earth and subdue it (Genesis 1:28) without a suitable companion, God created Eve. Human procreation, as it is designed, takes place within the social framework.

Being fruitful, multiplying, and filling the earth are all social interaction indicators. Even subduing the earth implies responsibilities one man, alone, cannot accomplish.

We can only surmise that there was harmony between Adam and Eve until the serpent came along. It is the nature of God to be with two people in agreement on earth: *For where two or three are gathered together in my name, there am I in the midst of them* (Matthew 18:19, 20 KJV). In Genesis 3:8, we read that God walked in the garden in the evening. While scripture does not explicitly say that was His habit, it does not seem plausible that He would take a stroll in Adam's domain after he had disobeyed and not before.

Until the serpent tempted Eve, it seems that Adam, Eve, and God interacted socially and were in agreement. Let me remind you of the power in the interdependent triune God and the reflection of that relationship in man, made in His image, body, spirit, and soul. As if to imitate this phenomenon, social power is at its strongest when three agree:

> *Two are better than one, in that their cooperative efforts yield this advantage: if one of them falls, the other will help his partner up—woe to him who is alone when he falls and has no one to help him up. Again, if two people sleep together, they keep each other warm; but how can one person be warm by himself? Moreover, an attacker may defeat someone who is alone, but two can resist him; and a three-stranded cord is not easily broken.*

Ecclesiastes 4:9-12

Application

Just as spiritual, intellectual, and psychological wellness dictate physical fitness, optimum social wellness depends on physical health. Our physical condition influences all our actions and interactions. When we are unwell, those with whom we interact are required, and often expected, to accommodate our deficiencies. Our government passes laws to ensure provisions for the unhealthy. We have become so accustomed to the aging process we no longer see it as abnormal. We prepare for it, save for it, build unique communities to accommodate it, sacrifice time and energy to take care of it, and take those who are not prepared to follow the rules governing the process to court to force them to do it. We have designed a social lifestyle around the unnatural condition of aging and dying that drains our finances and makes the healthcare industry rich.

In our ignorance of God's provision for total health, we have renovated our social systems. They no longer reflect God's plan for true prosperity. We have learned to die, and in many cases, prefer death to what we now consider life. Our churches promote programs to care for the dying rather than focusing on the power in God's provision for life (John 10:10).

Occupational Health

Definition of Occupation
An activity in which one engages; the principal business of one's life.

Perspective

Our occupational health is an expression of how we do what we do. Scripture instructs us to do everything we do in love (I Corinthians. 16:14). Interestingly, the most common use of the word love is in the context of agreement. It is only in agreement that we can *let the Word of the Messiah, in all its richness, live in us, as we teach and counsel each other in all wisdom, and as we sing psalms, hymns and spiritual songs with gratitude to God in our hearts. That is, everything we do or say, we do in the name of the Lord Yeshua, giving thanks through Him to God the Father* (Colossians 3:16-18).

As we occupy ourselves in our homes, churches, schools, businesses, communities, government, and interaction with other societies, God intends that we act according to the love of Jesus, the Messiah (Colossians 3:16). Anything less than that restricts occupational health. How we conduct ourselves in each of these areas is pervasive. The trickle-down effect, a term often used in economics, explains the phenomenon seen when something new appears in the marketplace. When new products come on the market, they are usually high-priced. Only the wealthy can afford them. Over time, the price decreases, and the general public can buy them.

I like to think of doing all we do in the name of the Lord Jesus in that way. At first, when we are the only ones buying into that concept, the price we pay may be high. But, as others buy in, it becomes the norm, and more people adopt it. Eventually, a way of life that once set us apart becomes the foundation of a society. In this way, occupational health is pervasive, replacing old patterns that lead to death instead of life:

The house of the wicked will be destroyed, but the tent of the upright will flourish. There can be a way which seems right to a person, but at its end are the ways of death.

Proverbs 13:11,12

Application

Once again, we need to consider our core values. In Jim Lupkin's book, *Predictive Social Media: A Guide to Mastering Core Values, Relationships, and a Disruptive System That Is Changing the World of Business*, he admonishes his readers to master the blend of core values, relationships, and systems, and we'll experience swift and life-altering success.[7] He speaks to his business-minded readers, but the premise applies to how we occupy ourselves in every way. The blend of core values, relationships, and systems we must master for success brings us back to the understanding that the seven dimensions of health overlap. They are inseparable.

Jim's emphasis on authentic relationships and the importance of an individual's core values directing what she does, speaks to everything we have already considered here. How we conduct ourselves is an expression of who we are. Who we are is an expression of our relationship with God in three persons—Father, Son, and Holy Spirit. As a reflection of Him, *we can be confident of this very thing, that he who hath begun a good work in you will perform it until the day of Jesus Christ* (Philippians 1:6).

...for God is the one working among you both the willing and the working for what pleases him. Do everything without kvetching or arguing, so that you may be blameless and pure children of God, without defect in the midst of a twisted and perverted generation, among whom you shine like stars in the sky, as you hold on to the Word of Life.

Philippians 2:13-15

Environmental Health

Definition of Environment

*The circumstances, objects, or conditions by which one is sur-
rounded; the complex of physical, chemical, and biotic factors (such
as climate, soil, and living things) that act upon an organism or an
ecological community and ultimately determine its form and survival; the aggregate of social and cultural conditions that influence the
life of an individual or community.*

Perspective

In its most uncomplicated form, the definition of environment can
be *the circumstances, objects, or conditions surrounding a person,
place, or thing.* That idea is self-limiting. As I sit here writing, I can
describe my environment reasonably easily: I am safe, comfortable,
secure, and free to do what I am doing without untoward demands
I cannot meet. If I limit this discussion to what I can see and understand, I don't have to concern myself too much.

The second part of the dictionary definition is a bit more trouble-
some: *the complex combination of physical, chemical, and biotic
factors (such as climate, soil, and living things) that act upon an
organism or an ecological community and ultimately determine its
form and survival.* So, if I am going to concern myself with that definition, I will have to do some research. It is undoubtedly complex. I
won't be able to look around and relax because I don't see or feel
anything that concerns me about my environment. There are un-
deniably complex factors I can't see or feel acting upon me—even
items in my home that I take for granted.

Then there is that final description: *the aggregate of social and cultural conditions that influence the life of an individual or community.*
The word *aggregate* means the whole sum or amount: everything
that affects me amassed together to doom me to failure or propel
me toward success. Either I don't stand a chance or Glory Be to
God, I've Got This!

I choose **Glory Be to God!** No matter what the environmentalists
say, this world is not going to hell in a handbasket. I have God's

Word on that and the Holy Spirit to make sure we humans don't destroy God's creation, no matter how hard we try. Read what Romans 8:26-30 says:

Similarly, the Spirit helps us in our weakness; for we don't know how to pray the way we should. But the Spirit himself pleads on our behalf with groanings too deep for words; and the one who searches hearts knows exactly what the Spirit is thinking, because his pleadings for God's people accord with God's will. Furthermore, we know that God causes everything to work together for the good of those who love God and are called in accordance with his purpose; because those whom he knew in advance, he also determined in advance would be conformed to the pattern of his Son, so that he might be the firstborn among many brothers; and those whom he thus determined in advance, he also called; and those whom he called, he also caused to be considered righteous; and those whom he caused to be considered righteous he also glorified!

Application

Don't misunderstand me. I believe we must be good stewards of what God has given us. The world as we know it shows clear signs of abuse. In his ill-gotten knowledge of good and evil, that abuse has occurred as man has misused what God intended to be our safe haven on earth. Had Adam—and Eve—eaten the fruit of the Tree of Life as God commanded, the earth would not now be crying out.

The creation waits eagerly for the sons of God to be revealed; for the creation was made subject to frustration—not willingly, but because of the one who subjected it. But it was given a reliable hope that it too would be set free from its bondage to decay and would enjoy the freedom accompanying the glory that God's children will have. We know that until now, the whole creation has been groaning as with the pains of childbirth.

Romans 8:19-22

Our environment has suffered, and we are experiencing less than true prosperity in our current state. It is not God's intention for us to remain in this condition during our time on earth. It is wonderful to be able to look forward to the home the Messiah has gone to prepare for us (John 14:1-2), but He sent the Holy Spirit to pre-pare us for that event. As we become confident of His plan for true prosperity in the seven dimensions of health and submit ourselves to that plan, fully expecting the promised results, we will begin to profit from God's wisdom. Our use of the resources on this earth will change. Our use of the talents He has given us will change, and our care for each other will change. His Kingdom will come and be done in earth (in us) as it is in heaven. As it does, we will keep His name holy (Matthew 6:9-13).

In its original state, our environment was created to express a triune God and His plan for true prosperity. We can see that plan in what has been termed The Seven Dimensions of Health. There is nothing spiritual or supernatural about that concept. It is simply an organized way of explaining a complicated model that defies natu-ral understanding—an example of our intellect at work.

Glory be to God!

Our Helper, the Holy Spirit, cultivates our confidence as we allow Him to hover over the darkness that covers our soul—just as He did in Genesis in preparation for God, the Father (YAHWEH), to say, *Light be!* That Light, Jesus, the Son, overcomes our less-than condition and restores us to fellowship with the Father. In that con-dition of wholeness, we experience what it means to eat the fruit of the Tree of Life—and our lives reflect true prosperity in the seven dimensions of health.

Endnotes

1. Hettler, Bill, MD. n.d. *Origin of the Hettler Model of Wellness: Balance the Six Dimensions of your life.* Accessed 8 10, 2022. https://www.hettler.com/.

2. Vocabulary.com: Dictionary: holy. A division of IXL Learning. https://www.vocabulary.com/dictionary/

3. Carpenter, Glen. 2012. GOD'S NUMBERS - A Study Guide in Bible Symbolism. Kindle Edition

4. Vine, W.E., Unger, Merrill F. and White Jr., William. 1996. *Vine's Complete Expository Dictionary of Old and New Testament Words.* Nashville, TN: T. Nelson

5. 2007-2022. *GoodTherapyBlog: psychPediaP Psyche.* LLC GoodTherapy. Accessed 8 16, 2022. https://www.goodtherapy.org/blog/psychpedia/psyche.

6. Purdom, Georgia, Dr., Menton, David, Dr. 2010. *Ancient Biblical Lifespans: Did Adam Live Over 900 Years?* https://answersingenesis.org/bible-timeline/genealogy/did-adam-and-noah-really-live-over-900-years/

7. Lupkin, Jim. *Predictive Social Media: A Guide to Mastering Core Values, Relationships, and a Disruptive System That Is Changing the World of Business.2020* Kindle Edition. SPOV Publishing

Definitions throughout the chapter: Merriam-Webster Online Dictionary copyright © 2022 by Merriam-Webster, Incorporated https://www.merriam-webster.com/dictionary/

Ellen Boyer has reinvented herself every time life has presented the opportunity. Her 2-part contribution to this anthology, Experiencing True Prosperity in the Seven Dimensions of Health, demonstrates her latest version of herself—a healthier, energetic 81-year-old writer.

Ellen's years of experience in community living, ministry, Bible study, and teaching form the foundation of what she terms a disruptive force in the "normal" flow of traditional thinking. She intends to "shake the tree" of lackadaisical Bible reading patterns to discover God's plan for true prosperity. A Master's degree and career in IT support and management in the legal, accounting, and medical fields have offered ample opportunity to sharpen her communication skills. In addition, seven years of living and working in Germany with travel opportunities throughout the European Union increased her love of God's creation everywhere.

Ellen freely admits she is her own best audience, and she would write to entertain herself. But instead, her desire to awaken today's Christian women to the reality of God's provision for prosperity drives her to write for you. You are the women who will produce the change we can expect as we humble ourselves in sight of the Lord, and He lifts us up.

https://www.facebook.com/groups/prosperbih

Chapter 13

The Rewards of Confidence in God

Dr. Lana Wynn Scroggins

*So do not throw away your confidence; it will be richly rewarded.
You need to persevere so that when you have done the will of God,
you will receive what he has promised.*

Hebrews 10:35-36 (NIV)

- What part of your life is uncertain right now?
- Are you persevering, confident that God will care for you?
- Which rewards of confidence in God have you recognized through challenging times in your life?

Homeless—the First Time

Confidence in My Provider

Suddenly, all seemed lost. For the first time in my fifty-one years of living on this earth, I was homeless. Well, if you count the first year of my life in foster care, then this was technically the second time I needed God to provide a place to call home—but that's a different story for another time.

I'd lived with a family for over six years. I cared for their children, their pets, and their home. They gave me a roof over my head, and I worked hard to do my part. But over time, the dynamics in the home changed. One night in 2006, God said it was time to go. I trusted Him to help me find a new home, so I put a few belongings in my suitcase, took my purse with almost $100, and drove my truck to a friend's house for the night.

The next day, I met with my pastor to share my story. I told him my crazy plan to get enough money to go home, convince Mom to give me the retired camper trailer resting in the back of the hayfield, and get a job. He gave me his prayers and $400, and sent me on my way.

I set out for the thirteen-hour drive home that day by myself, not knowing what the future would hold. While I'd never been homeless before, loneliness was an intimate companion I'd known since childhood. Due to some circumstances of my childhood, I walked through life, wounded and lost for decades, until God saved me. Now, with each passing mile, I came closer to the old farmhouse and all of its memories. But God had provided for me before, so I drove in peace, trusting He'd do it again. He had to.

As I prayed my way home, I remembered Abraham. God also sent him on a journey to an unknown future. Abraham remained steadfast in God's promises, even when all seemed lost. As Abraham persevered, God provided a home and the seemingly impossible promise of a son who would begin a lineage as numerous as the stars that now lighted my way to Mom's house. Abraham's trust in God gave him confidence in God's provision right up to the moment he raised a knife over his son. Abraham then persevered to become the father of nations. Just as God provided a ram in the thicket to save Abraham's son, I trusted God with my tomorrow, too.

Steadfast Faith in Trials

As I pulled into the driveway of the old farmhouse, I could see past the barn to the back corner of the hayfield where the dilapidated camper rested under the shade trees. My adoptive father had passed away many years prior, but Mom came outside to greet me, followed by her new husband, my brother, and his friend. I told them my story and asked her husband if I could have his camper. They hadn't used it but once or twice each summer to go to the lake, so he said if I could move it, I could have it.

I knew my sturdy truck could pull the camper, but I'd never thought about how I'd move it. My brother hooked up the camper to my truck, only to find that the camper's rear brake lights didn't work. The two men worked for what seemed like forever, until they decided the field mice must have chewed through the wires. Without brake lights, pulling the camper through the Ozark Mountains wasn't an option. They drove away to leave me in the driveway with my childhood memories and a home I couldn't live in.

That's when I had a little fit. Everyone had left. There was no one around for miles. I went out to the middle of the hayfield where it was just me and God. I threw my hands up in the air and yelled at Him. I don't know why I thought I needed to yell at God—I'm sure he can hear without me yelling, but I guess I just needed to rant. I prayed, "I don't know how we're going to make this work, but it's got to. This is my chance to have my own home, to be on my own. We've come this far. I trust You and I know this doesn't end here, even though everyone else has left. This camper has to work, God. It just has to!"

I yelled and prayed earnestly to God for about fifteen minutes before heading back to the house. I didn't know what I was going to do, but I wasn't about to give up. A few minutes later, my brother called and said that he and his friend might have figured out what was wrong. They were coming back to the farm to try again.

When the brake lights came on, I cried, "Thank You, Jesus!" and jumped into the truck. My brother met me at the driver's side window and asked, "Have you ever pulled a camper before?" Once again, I hadn't even thought about it, so my brother spent most of the afternoon teaching me how to pull the camper until he decided I was ready for the trip over the mountains. I was about to leave when my mom handed me a little money and said, "This should help until you get a job. I hope you don't need more."

Peace in the Journey

By the time I reached the mountain, it was almost dark. It would be a long, winding drive, but I wasn't worried. God was with me. I kept both the truck and camper on the narrow road, even through pouring rain and where there was no guardrail between me and the valley below.

I reached the bottom of the mountain and continued to Birmingham. I'd heard Walmart allowed people to park campers overnight for free, so I pulled into the first Walmart store I saw. I didn't have electricity, so I bought a small lantern and a few other supplies.

I spent my first rainy night in my own home parked in a Walmart parking lot. I had no electricity, one suitcase of belongings, and a few hundred dollars to my name. I had no idea where I would look for a job tomorrow or where I'd park the camper. But as I lay down for the night, my only thought was of how God had cared for Moses and the Israelites day-by-day. I thanked Jesus for the safe drive and for a place to call my own, and fell asleep peacefully, confident He would provide for my tomorrow, too.

What part of your life is uncertain right now? Are you confident that God will care for you? **Persevere**

The Rewards of Perseverance

I woke up and called a few friends to tell them I was in town and looking for a job. My friend Ed said I could park the camper on his property until I found my own lot. One of my friends invited me to join them on the soccer field. As soon as I got to the soccer field, a friend told me they were looking for a physical education teacher at their Christian school. I told her I had a college degree in physical education, and I would be glad to be their PE teacher.

The next day when I showed up for work, the school principal and pastor of the church told me he'd learned that one of his church members had an empty lot they could rent for a very reasonable price. So now I had a camper, a job, and a home. Within a few days, God took me from sudden homelessness and gave me a safe home and a job.

I'd learned many years prior that God was always with me in the fire, making sure I didn't get burned. He held back the waves, so I didn't drown, just like He did for the Israelites crossing the Red

Sea. I don't remember ever doubting that God wasn't helping me all along the way. I knew that He would provide, and He rewarded my growing confidence in Him by giving me peace in the journey and everything I needed.

But that's not where this story ends.

Homeless—Again

Confidence through Cancer

God continued to care for me, always providing, and my confidence in Him continued to grow. It was just me and God doing life. So, when I was diagnosed with stage four breast cancer in 2018, I knew He wouldn't leave me.

I got really sick because my right lung filled with fluid from the cancer cells. I spent three weeks in the hospital with pneumonia, and the cancer cells had to be drained from my lungs at least every week.

Peace Through the Storm

It was October 2018 when the National Weather Service first issued severe storm warnings, followed by hurricane warnings, and finally recommendations to evacuate. Hurricane Michael promised to be one of the worst storms the area had ever known. Authorities expected power would go down for weeks and many homes would be destroyed.

I took my doctor's advice to stay with friends in another state with a good hospital nearby. I packed up everything I could fit in my car in case the storm destroyed my trailer. And indeed, Michael was upgraded to a category five hurricane. I watched on TV as the storm destroyed everything. I got a sad feeling in the pit of my stomach; I knew my life was about to change again.

But when you go through something one time and it comes around again, it's easier to remain faithful, believing that God will help everything turn out okay. God built my confidence in Him through the first time I was homeless, so I knew He would build my confidence in Him even more this time.

The area was declared a federal disaster. Many of my friends lost everything, and I returned to find the top of my trailer was blown off. I salvaged what belongings I could and stayed with friends for a few weeks until the power could be restored.

Food and supplies were provided through a distribution center at church, but I needed help. Mom helped the last time I was homeless, so I reached out to her again. She was older now, so she needed help to be able to help me. God used her, my cousins, and a few friends to help restore what was lost.

Steadfastness through Loss

It wasn't as quick or easy as it was last time. I walked in faith for weeks, just going about my life. God provided for me the last time I was homeless, and I just knew He'd do it again. He'd make it all work out; He just had to.

As supply shortages, land zoning, and paperwork lingered, I got frustrated. I remember once again standing in the middle of my friend's yard praying to God. It's possible I may have yelled at Him a little, too. I still don't know why I thought I needed to yell, but somehow, I guess I must have thought He could hear my plea if I talked loud enough.

I felt like I was at the end of my rope, and I told my friend, "I'm about to lose my faith—I don't know if I can stand one more day of this!" She said, "Oh, no, no, no, no, you can't lose your faith. We need you to have your faith because your faith is strength for us. We lean on your faith. We have to get this fixed—now!"

Just like God used others to help me last time, my friend made a few phone calls, and I had my lot ready to go soon after. Looking back, I have no doubt God had it all under control. God was there the whole way saying, "It's all going to work out."

The Rewards of Confidence in God

Hebrews 10:35-36 tells us to hold on to our confidence in God because we need this confidence to persevere through His will, and then we will receive the rich reward He promised. I've learned that the rewards of confidence in God are faith, steadfastness, peace, and perseverance.

Faith and Trust

---

*Confidence is faith in our Provider,
and it is trusting that God will never leave us.*

Hebrews 11:1 says that faith is confidence in what we hope for and trusting in what we can't see. Confidence is faith and trust. Even when I couldn't see it, I trusted God would provide a home and a job. Confidence is faith in our Provider, and it is trusting that God will never leave us. Faith is when we know that we know He will make it all work out.

Each time we overcome through God's grace, He adds fuel to our tank, building up confidence that He will be with us in the fire, that He will hold back the waters so we don't drown. We just need to remember that He loves us so much that He gave His only Son so we would have eternal life with Him.

Steadfastness

Steadfastness is a firm, immovable belief.[1] Steadfastness in the face of difficulty is fueled by our confidence in God. I firmly believed God would take care of me, even when I was yelling at Him. When I was faced with homelessness the first time, my steadfastness grew alongside my confidence in God, so I just knew it was going to work out when I faced both cancer and a longer homelessness the next time.

Peace

The reward of trusting Him is that He will give us peace, lead us in the right path, bring us joy, and be with us forever and ever. Even when I had no idea where I would sleep the next day, I wasn't afraid. I had an occasional yelling fit, but I didn't sit and cry in my camper all day. I had peace because I just knew it was going to happen. My steadfast confidence in God gave me great peace and joy, knowing He will always be there to take good care of me.

Perseverance

The key word in Hebrews 10:35-36 is *persevere*.[2] To persevere means to endure, to continue in a course of action even in the face of difficulty or with little or no prospect of success.

Our confidence and faith in God are built each time we endure and keep going to overcome each task in the face of all obstacles.

In the Bible, no matter what Joseph went through, he knew God would provide. Whether he was in the pit, the palace, or the prison, Joseph knew God had a plan, and he didn't give up. Joseph's confidence in God gave him a steadfast faith to remain peaceful in all trials, and Joseph's reward for his perseverance was leadership of the entire kingdom and a reconciled family.

Our confidence and faith in God are built each time we endure and keep going to overcome each task in the face of all obstacles. I could have just given up, but I didn't. I just kept moving forward, knowing God would make something happen. If at any point along the way had I had given up, I would not have made it to the right time and place to see God's provision for a home come true.

An Endless Gift

My confidence in God fueled my immovable faith, which then gave me peace to make better decisions so I could persevere. God builds our confidence in Him every time we persevere. In this way, confidence in God is a self-perpetuating cycle, so trusting in Him is its own reward. I won't say it always comes naturally, but sometimes it's all I've got.

God gives you everything you ask that aligns with His will. Certainly, He wants you to have ever-increasing confidence in Him, steadfast faith, peace, and perseverance.

Praise Him for what He's brought you through and ask Him to continue building your confidence in Him a little bit each day.

> *So do not throw away your confidence; it will be richly rewarded.*
> *You need to persevere so that when you have done the will of God,*
> *you will receive what he has promised.*

Hebrews 10:35-36 (NIV)

Endnotes

1, 2. https://www.merriam-webster.com/dictionary/

Dr. Lana Wynn Scroggins is a writer and speaker who is passionate about sharing Jesus with others. She's found personal healing and steadfast hope in the pages of God's Word. Lana's love for Jesus led her to create Giving Jesus (https://givingjesus.com), centered around a place to find inspiration, motivation, and encouragement to help support you in the good times and the times when you need encouragement the most.

Lana delights in living in her small coastal community, living by the water and walking on the beach. Her days are centered on her faith, her business Giving Jesus, and writing her books. Her favorite pastime is coloring and creating her craft projects. Lana has a unique way of journaling and sharing God's Word with hand drawing the journal pages.

Lana has a BA degree in Physical Education and was a teacher for Faith Christian School. She also has a BS, MS and a PhD in Information Technology.

Lana is the author of many books including activity books for adults and children along with devotional studies for women. She is passionate about her writing and sharing Jesus through her books. She also shares her devotional studies with her church home group and her devotional Facebook group called Your Devotional Journey.

Her favorite quote to live by is by Babe Ruth: "Every strike brings me closer to the next home run."

https://givingjesus.com/

Navigating the Trials of Life
with Confidence

Dear Reader,

Most of this Book 1 in the *Cultivating Confidence from the Lord* series focuses on convictions we need from the Lord in life. A huge portion of this book centers on the work and ministry we do, because it is written by members of the National Association of Christian Women Entrepreneurs. We love to talk about our work and service and we need help navigating the waters.

In our Introduction you read that we are writing a series of chapters and books about Cultivating Confidence from the Lord

- in life,
- through trials, and
- as entrepreneurs.

We're considering a book for young adults and one for children as well.

Trials, Losses, and Transitions

I've worked with grieving families and families in crisis since 1995, as a pastoral counselor and licensed professional counselor in different ministry settings and in private practice. I've remarked so many times that grief work has been a very solid foundation on which to build counseling ministry, because everyone who sits across from the professional counselor, lay counselor, or pastoral counselor—even those sitting across from you in your living room who are suffering— are grieving a loss of some kind. Perhaps they've experienced death or separation, or at the very least believe that life hasn't turned out as they hoped and they need someone to talk to about it. In the same vein, almost everyone who sits before us is struggling through a transition of some sort, and while they may not label it as a loss or bereavement, it is challenging nonetheless.

So we want you to understand that we included one chapter in this anthology on cultivating confidence from the Lord during transitions to introduce a forthcoming book in the *Cultivating Confidence From the Lord* series of anthologies based on suffering trials. It is our hope that the book will be written by Biblical counselors across the world. Look for that anthology, as it will include chapters about needing confidence from the Lord through various trials—such as through self-discovery and self-improvement; in understanding feelings, values, and worth; for peacekeeping and peacemaking; for forgiveness; through difficult life events that cause grief, bereavement, and loss—such as the death of a loved one, job loss, physical illness, conflict, and conflict resolution; through mental health issues—such as pride, fear and worry, desire, abuse, addictions and compulsion, anxiety and panic, anger, boundaries, depression, guilt and shame, habits and behaviors, narcissism, and stress; and understanding the will of God through transitions and decision making, like the transition through college and career or from corporate to entrepreneurship, marriage relationships and parenting, semi-retirement and retirement (or "re-firement"), and more. In what other challenges of life do you need confidence?

I hope you'll be blessed by this next sample chapter from a future book in the Cultivating Confidence from the Lord series.

Chapter 14

Navigating Life Transitions with Confidence - With Wings Like Eagles

Karen Lindwall-Bourg

*Yet those who wait for the Lord
Will gain new strength;
They will mount up with wings like eagles,
They will run and not get tired,
They will walk and not become weary.*

Isaiah 40:31 (NASB)

The title of the 40th chapter of Isaiah in the New American Standard Bible is "The Greatness of God." I don't know about you, but during uncertain times and in times of waiting while transitioning from one season to another, I'm not usually focusing on the greatness of God. I am focusing on my own journey.

Even transitions you desire—college, marriage, children, or a new work position—can be fraught with uncertainties and challenges. And it's okay to acknowledge that!

So, how do you navigate these transitions with confidence from the Lord? Are you navigating a life transition right now? Actually, are you ever NOT navigating a shift in life?

- Is this current life transformation causing you a bit (or a lot a bit) of angst?
- Are you waiting (with baited breath or troubled heart) before the Lord for His answers to your questions about this transition?

- Do you desire more confidence as you step forward into His Will for this time of refashioning?
- In the shifting, transforming, and refashioning, is the Lord your confidence?

Transition Of, To, and From

Looking at the dictionary definition of transitions, you repeatedly read the words transition *of*, transition *to*, transition *from*. You might experience a transition *of* power in your workplace. You might experience a transition *from* your first apartment. You might experience a transition *to* or direction to a new home. There is a period or phase and a change or shift from one state, subject, or place to another. There's an obvious connection or link within the of, the to, and the from. A passage or a bridge, if you will.[1]

Transitioning to and from implies progress. I like that!

But I'm a glass half-empty gal, learning to be a glass half-full gal—so I often see transitions, because they are challenging, as antithetical to progress—as taking more steps backward than forward.

Antonyms for the word transition include *same, beginning, still, stay put.* Even when you know you need to make some changes and grow, staying put sometimes feels safer. It's become your comfort zone.

Additional antonyms for the word transition are *stagnate and stalemate,* which seem to imply there is an opposing force to moving forward. That doesn't feel comfortable at all.

Another antonym for the word transition is *waiting.* I wrote a note to myself as I was searching for God's view of transitions, wanting to remember that waiting is a very Biblical, godly stance, and I was immediately led to Isaiah 40:31.

144

> *Yet those who wait for the Lord*
> *Will gain new strength;*
> *They will mount up with wings like eagles,*
> *They will run and not get tired,*
> *They will walk and not become weary.*

I'm more inclined to think of transitions as a passive process. Something that is happening to me. Another glass half empty view.

Does God see transitions that way?

Look at His words of action in that verse—*wait, gain, mount, run, walk*. These are some of the most intensely active words I've ever heard. And with God's promise that I will mount up with wings as eagles, I am greatly encouraged.

> *Our goal, as we cultivate confidence from the Lord*
> *is to transition our heartset and mindset about transitions in life*
> *so that they align more with the way God sees transitions in life.*

Synonyms for the word *transition* are numerous and include descriptions:

- hinting at minor changes—adjustment, alteration, modification, shift, substitution, variation;
- implying major changes—changeover, conversion, deformation, disfigurement, displacement, distortion, mutation, replacement, supplantation, transmutation. (Some of these words sound downright painful!) I especially like this synonym—metamorphosis.

Consider the miraculous process of egg, larva, caterpillar, pupae or cocoon, butterfly—a transition only a majestic God can perform. There is very little resemblance, if any at all, between a caterpillar and a butterfly. And yet after this majestic and complete meta-morphosis, they still share the same DNA, it's just rearranged and expressed differently. Even more astounding, somewhere in the middle of this transformative transition, if you cut open a cocoon, you can find a sort of gooey primordial soup that doesn't remotely resemble either the caterpillar or the butterfly.

In the same way, your transitions may feel dramatically transform-ing, and with that comes fear and doubt about growing forward. After all, what does that mean and what will be the end result? You and I cannot see fully as God sees. And yet, you can trust Him with the whole journey.

- Transfiguration may remind you of Jesus' transfiguration before His crucifixion. What glory!
- Transformation—you may actually hear the emphatic words "total transformation."
- *re* words suggesting *again* and *anew*—reconstruction, re-conversion, redo, redoing, refashioning, reformation, re-making, remodeling, revamping, revision, reworking

There is absolutely nothing passive about these words. You can almost feel the intention and purpose and action behind their mean-ings. God is working in your waiting. You have some work to do as well.

God is Working in Your Waiting through Transitions.

God is working in your waiting. You have some work to do as well.

You could probably not adequately list all of the transitions you ex-perience from the beginning to the end of your life. Some of these transitions are sought or anticipated, some are a natural part of growing, some are unexpected or unanticipated, and some are diffi-cult. Are any of them easy? Even life transitions that you don't think of as traumatic events, that you chose and planned for yourself, are often accompanied by at least some challenges. Transitions are universal to us all but also very unique experiences for each of us.

I personally tend to think of transitions as traumatic events, and when I look at Biblical transitions—the creation of the world, the parting of the Red Sea, births, deaths, and more—they seem tragically beautiful or beautifully tragic. They are difficult and sometimes violent. I can't recall a Bible story that ends with, "and it was very easy."

There is a universal *dis-ease* of waiting. We hate waiting for what we want, no matter how mature we think we are.

So, what does God teach you about the transitions of life?

How is God working in your waiting through transitions?

The Lord is Your Confidence; Respond to Him.

Transitions should cause you to turn to God, to go deeper, to ask God, "What are You doing? Where are You leading me? What are You teaching me?"

You approach these questions with both confidence and caution.

You are cautious because you know your tendency is to want to know causes and reasons and timing, to do anything that relieves the waiting and the trial of transitions.

You are confident because He is always with you through every transition.

The Lord speaks to us about everything we need for *life and godliness* through transitions.

> *Grace and peace be multiplied to you in the knowledge of God and of Jesus our Lord; seeing that His divine power has granted to us everything pertaining to life and godliness, through the true knowledge of Him who called us by His own glory and excellence.*
> 2 Peter 1:2, 3 (NASB)

In times of transition when you feel distress, I want to encourage you to respond to God with confidence.

I want to inspire confidence by reminding you that God speaks to you.

I want to embolden you to respond to Him by prompting you to stop and listen. **He speaks to you.**

I want your responses to be ordered in such a way that it is apparent each response builds upon the other, becomes stronger or more active, more passionate.

He will never leave us or forsake us. He is always with us through every transition.

Walk this journey of confidence through transitions with me.

Meditate on one of these confidences each day.

The Lord is your confidence.

*For the Lord will be your Confidence
and will keep your
foot from being caught.*

Proverbs 3:26

You respond to Him.

I can do all things through Christ who strengthens me.

Philippians 4:13

Jesus assures you.

In God's sovereign wisdom, transitions are expected. In the world you have tribulation, but take courage; I have overcome the world.

John 16:33b

You hope in Him

The Lord delights in those who fear him, who put their hope in his unfailing love.

Psalm 147:11

God sees you.

Then she [Hagar] called the name of the Lord who spoke to her, "You are a God who sees"; for she said, "Have I even remained alive here after seeing Him?" Therefore the well was called Beer-lahai-roi [the well of the Living One Who sees me]; behold, it is between Kadesh and Bered.

Genesis 16:13-14

You remember He sees you.
You are seen!

Keep me as the apple of Your eye; Hide me in the shadow of Your wings,

Psalm 17:8

He hears you.

For I know the plans that I have for you,' declares the Lord, 'plans for welfare and not for calamity to give you a future and a hope. Then you will call upon Me and come and pray to Me, and I will listen to you. You will seek Me and find Me when you search for Me with all your heart. I will be found by you,' declares the Lord, 'and I will restore your fortunes and will gather you from all the nations and from all the places where I have driven you,' declares the Lord,

Jeremiah 29:11-14a

You remember He hears you.

You are heard.
You are a child of God, a saint who has been brought near;
you are even called a friend of God.

(v. 12)... you will call upon Me and come and pray
to Me, and I will listen to you. '
declares the Lord,

Jeremiah 29:11-14a

Jesus teaches you to pray.

And he said unto them, When ye pray, say,
Our Father which art in heaven, Hallowed be thy name.
Thy kingdom come. Thy will be done, as in heaven, so in earth.
Give us day by day our daily bread. And forgive us our sins;
for we also forgive every one that is indebted to us.
And lead us not into temptation; but deliver us from evil.

Luke 11:2-4 (KJV)

You say something. Say anything.

When you struggle to pray, you just don't know the words
to pray, or you feel too overwhelmed to pray, you choose
just one word to focus on, like peace, grace or strength.

You remember He intercedes for you!

Christ Jesus is He who died, yes, rather who was raised, who is at the
right hand of God, who also intercedes for us.

Romans 8:34

He has given precious and magnificent promises.

For by these He has granted to us His precious and magnificent promises, so that by them you may become partakers of the divine nature, having escaped the corruption that is in the world...

2 Peter 1:4

You are emboldened and assured by His promises. Amen!

For as many as are the promises of God, in Him they are yes; therefore also through Him is our Amen to the glory of God through us.

2 Corinthians 1:20

He speaks to you.

Behold, I stand at the door and knock; if anyone hears My voice and opens the door, I will come in to him and will dine with him, and he with Me.

Revelation 3:20

I pray you will hear when God speaks your name.

You stop and listen. You seek God's heart. You draw close to Him through prayer, time in the Word, asking for wisdom and asking to hear Him in unique ways.

My sheep hear My voice, and I know them, and they follow Me; and I give eternal life to them, and they will never perish; and no one will snatch them out of My hand.

John 10:27-28

When God speaks your name, it gets your attention. When God speaks your name, you surely know who you are—or who you are meant to become.

He is with you.

Do not fear, for I am with you;
Do not anxiously look about you, for I am your God.
I will strengthen you,
Surely I will help you,
Surely I will uphold you with My righteous right hand.

Isaiah 41:10

You pour out your heart before Him.

Trust in Him at all times, O people;
Pour out your heart before Him;
God is a refuge for us. Selah.

Psalm 62:8

God forgives.

If we confess our sins, he is faithful and just to forgive
us our sins and to cleanse us from all unrighteousness.

1 John 1:9

You simply open the door.

His forgiveness is yours when you simply open the door.
Invite Him in. Confess to Him. Accept His cleansing forgiveness.

1 John 1:9

God the Father comforts you.

Blessed be the God and Father of our Lord Jesus Christ, the Father of
mercies and God of all comfort, who comforts us in all our affliction so
that we will be able to comfort those who are in any affliction with the
comfort with which we ourselves are comforted by God.

2 Corinthians 1:3-4

You comfort and are comforted.

You listen to the wisdom of others who have endured hopeless
situations, ask for prayer and insights, and offer them comfort as well.

Jesus offers you rest.

Come to Me, all who are weary and heavy-laden, and I will give you rest. Take My yoke upon you and learn from Me, for I am gentle and humble in heart, and you will find rest for your souls. For My yoke is easy and My burden is light.

Matthew 11:28-30 (NASB)

Are you tired? Worn out? Burned out on religion? Come to me. Get away with me and you'll recover your life. I'll show you how to take a real rest. Walk with me and work with me—watch how I do it. **Learn the unforced rhythms of grace.** *I won't lay anything heavy or ill-fitting on you. Keep company with me and you'll learn to live freely and lightly.*

(The Message)

You rest in Him. You are at peace!

*In peace I will both lie down and sleep,
For You alone, O Lord, make me to dwell in safety.*

Psalm 4:8

The Lord is your HOPE.

"For I know the plans that I have for you," declares the Lord, "plans for welfare and not for calamity to give you a future and a hope."

Jeremiah 29:11

You are joyful and patient in waiting.
It is a time for a change within or work to be done.

…rejoicing in hope, persevering in tribulation, devoted to prayer,

Romans 12:12

For in hope we have been saved, but hope that is seen is not hope; for who hopes for what he already sees? But if we hope for what we do not see, with perseverance we wait eagerly [patiently - ESV] for it.

Romans 8:24

God is faithful.

God is faithful, through whom you were called into fellowship with His Son, Jesus Christ our Lord.

1 Corinthians 1:9

You remember (like Asaph in Psalm 77) what God has done in the past. He will do it again!

*Your faithfulness continues throughout all generations;
You established the earth,
and it stands [fast].*

Psalm 119:90

He loves you.

...for God is love. By this the love of God was manifested in us, that God has sent His only begotten Son into the world so that we might live through Him.

1 John 4:8b-9

He sent His Son for you! He reminds you that
you're loved, that He is at work on your behalf, that He is training
you to pray, to trust, to stand against every tactic of the enemy,
and He reminds you that He is Life.

You lean against Him.

Trust in the Lord with all your heart and do not lean on your own understanding. In all your ways acknowledge Him, and He will make your paths straight.

Proverbs 3:5-6

And when you reach the end of yourself and you're still waiting, there you are
leaning against God, entirely spent, and knowing He is with you always and
accepts you as you are because of Jesus.

You know that you are His!

God shelters you with His wings.
God shields you in the shadow of His wings.

Security of the One Who Trusts in the Lord.
He who dwells in the shelter of the Most High
Will abide in the shadow of the Almighty.
I will say to the Lord, "My refuge and my fortress,
My God, in whom I trust!"
For it is He who delivers you from the snare of the trapper
And from the deadly pestilence.
He will cover you with His pinions,
And under His wings you may seek refuge;
His faithfulness is a shield and bulwark.

Psalm 91:1-4

You are secure and humbled.

And under His wings you may seek refuge;
His faithfulness is a shield and bulwark.

Psalm 91:4b

Be gracious to me, O God, be gracious to me,
For my soul takes refuge in You;
And in the shadow of Your wings I will take refuge
Until destruction passes by.

Psalm 57:1

He fills you with joy and peace.

Now may the God of hope fill you with all joy and peace in believing,
so that you will abound in hope by the power of the Holy Spirit.

Romans 15:13

You sing with joy!

For You have been my help,
And in the shadow of Your wings
I sing for joy.

Psalm 63:7

God is powerful, and He is loving.

Ah Lord God! Behold, You have made the heavens and the earth by Your great power and by Your outstretched arm! Nothing is too difficult for You,...

Jeremiah 32:17

We have come to know and have believed the love which God has for us. God is love, and the one who abides in love abides in God, and God abides in him.

1 John 4:16

Believing God is loving means that there is care and purpose behind all that He does. He is faithful to help us right now and bring us blessings later. His judgment and timing are always perfectly good. He has promised to give us everything we need (Philippians 4:19).

You respond to Him with trust.
You move closer to fully and deeply trust Him, especially when during transitions, you don't have all the answers you desire.

Trust in the Lord with all your heart
And do not lean on your own understanding.
In all your ways acknowledge Him, and He will make your paths straight.

Proverbs 3:5-6

Even during that long road of silence, God cares deeply for you. You can be like David and remind yourself to

Wait for the Lord; be strong, and let your heart Take courage; wait for the Lord!

Psalm 27:14

God says, I am Over You.

He is Omnipresent - God is with you.
Proverbs 15:3; Job 31:4

Omnipotent - God is over you (Matthew 19:26) He is *powerful*. He is in charge of what's happening; things are not arbitrary or out of his control.
Omniscient - God knows all things (Proverbs 15:3; Job 31:4; Psalm 37:18; Psalm 44:21; Matthew 6:8; 1 John 3:20)
Omni-benevolent - God cares for you (Mark 10:18). He is *loving*; there is care and purpose behind all that He does.

You fear Him; you revere Him!

Who is like the Lord our God...
Psalm 113:5a

Therefore, since we receive a kingdom which cannot be shaken, let us show gratitude, by which we may offer to God an acceptable service with reverence and awe;
Hebrews 12:28

He bears you up.

Like an eagle that stirs up its nest, that flutters over its young, spreading out its wings, catching them, bearing them on its pinions,
Deuteronomy 32:11

You are blessed and you bless Him.

Every morning, look ahead and remember, "God will show me steadfast love today." And every evening, look back and declare His faithfulness.

Blessed be the Lord, who daily bears our burden, The God who is our salvation.
Psalm 68:19; Psalm 92

God works all things for your good.

And we know that God causes all things to work together for good to those who love God, to those who are called according to His purpose. For those whom He foreknew, He also predestined to become conformed to the image of His Son, so that He would be the firstborn among many brethren; and these whom He predestined, He also called; and these whom He called, He also justified; and these whom He justified, He also glorified.

Romans 8:28-30

You anticipate His answer.
You expect the unexpected, the supernatural.

We anticipate insight from the Lord! In just about any story in the Bible, there is a story of someone who feels like their situation is hopeless and then God comes in with a glorious hope and promise, and through ups and downs and twists and turns, He remains faithful to them all.

*God causes **all** things to work together for good to those who love God...*

Romans 8:28

My soul, wait thou only upon God; for my expectation is from him.

Psalm 62:6 (KJV)

He renews your strength.

But they that wait upon the Lord shall renew their strength; they shall mount up with wings as eagles; they shall run, and not be weary; and they shall walk, and not faint.

Isaiah 40:31 (KJV)

You soar!

Although you may struggle during transitions, place your hope in the Lord! You will soar aloft as with eagle's wings.

Like David, you can declare

For You are my lamp, O Lord;
And the Lord illumines my darkness.
For by You I can run upon a troop;
By my God I can leap [soar] over a wall.

2 Samuel 22:29-3

Wait Upon the Lord

Consider these wise words from Lori Roeleveld:

> In the waiting - God is present, active, and sustaining. There is always more happening than we can see. And in the waiting, we panic pray, we call on His name, we consider all possible outcomes, we pray with specificity, we praise, we pray scripture, we ask others to pray, we pray again. And when we reach the end of ourselves and we're still waiting, there you are, leaning against God, entirely spent; and He reminds you that you're loved; that He is at work on your behalf; that He is training you to pray, to trust, to stand against every tactic of the enemy. And He reminds you that He is life. Yes, others may meddle with your lowercase life, but no one can touch the uppercase Life He provides now and will provide into eternity. And you lean against Him, still waiting, but knowing He is with you always and accepts you as you are because of Jesus.[2]

Now to Him who is able to do far more abundantly beyond
all that we ask or think, according to the power that works within us,
to Him be the glory in the church and in Christ Jesus
to all generations forever and ever. Amen.

Ephesians 3:20 (NSAB)

God is Actively Working in Your Waiting

He has a purpose for every transition in your life. AND He Answers with Himself.

The Lord is NOT silent! The Lord knows what we need most during transitions, and it's not the certainty of an explanation; it is the certainty of knowing Him.

To cultivate confidence from the Lord and navigate life transitions with serenity, courage and wisdom, we respond rightly to Him as He answers with Himself.

May you always respond this way:

The Serenity Prayer

God, grant me the Serenity
To accept the things I cannot change...
Courage to change the things I can,
And Wisdom to know the difference.

Living one day at a time,
Enjoying one moment at a time,
Accepting hardship as the pathway to peace.
Taking, as He [Jesus] did, this sinful world as it is,
Not as I would have it.

Trusting that He will make all things right
if I surrender to His will.
That I may be reasonably happy in this life,
And supremely happy with Him forever in the next.

Amen.[3]

Cry out,
Answer with Yourself, Lord!
And, while You answer, I will wait for the Lord;
be strong, and let your heart take courage;
wait for the Lord!

Psalm 27:14 (ESV)

Endnotes

1. Merriam-Webster *Merriam-Webster.com dictionary*. https://www.merriam-webster.com/dictionary

2. Lori Roeleveld (Facebook post https://www.Facebook.com/ Lori roeleveld

3. The Serenity Prayer: Full Version (The Prayer Foundation) / Theologian Reinhold Neibuhr

About the Next Books in the Cultivating Confidence from the Lord Series

In this Book 1 of our Cultivating Confidence Series,

You read about gaining confidence

- through the wisdom of Proverbs;
- in your God-given calling;
- with a vision aligned with His;
- as you surrender to God's call;
- as you reframe your mindset;
- in the midst of warfare;
- with a confident crown;
- in financial stewardship and ownership;
- with newfound freedom;
- in God's plan for your prosperity through the seven dimensions of health;
- as you reap the rewards of confidence in God; and
- while navigating life transitions with confidence.

We have felt led from the beginning to continue writing on this subject in other books in the series.

Cultivating Confidence in LIFE

Under this banner, we'll talk about cultivating confidence in life to know God; to ask, seek, and knock when we need Him; to hear Him, believe Him, and obey Him; to understand His love for us; to invite Him in and ask with anticipation instead of expectation; to ask others for help; to accept the Lord's assignment for us, to be who He has called us to be and to do what He has called us to do; to align with His precepts; to assess our God-given calling or mandate and reaffirm that purpose frequently; to understand our identity in Christ; to build on our God-given strengths; to affirm everything through His word and His people; to live and work under grace; to rest in Him; to put on the whole armor of God to prepare; to act in faith, hope, love, and love for His people; to have an attitude of gratitude; to steward all He has entrusted to us; to make Him known; and to trust Him with the results of our life! Contact us if there is another area in which confidence is desired.

Now may the God of hope fill you with all joy and peace in believing, so that you will abound in hope by the power of the Holy Spirit.

Romans 15:13 (NASB)

Cultivating Confidence through TRIALS

Under this banner, we'll talk about needing confidence from the Lord through various trials such as through self-discovery and self-improvement; in understanding feelings, values, and worth; for peacekeeping and peacemaking; for forgiveness; through difficult life events that cause grief, bereavement, and loss such as the death of a loved one, job loss, physical illness, conflict, and conflict resolution; through mental health issues such as pride, fear and worry, desire, abuse, addictions and compulsion, anxiety and panic, anger, boundaries, depression, guilt and shame, habits and be-haviors, narcissism, and stress; and understanding the will of God through transitions and decision making, like the transition through college and career or from corporate to entrepreneurship, mar-riage relationships and parenting, semi-retirement and retirement (or "re-firement"), and more! In what other challenges of life do you need confidence? Feel free to reach out to us.

Therefore let us draw near with confidence to the throne of grace, so that we may receive mercy and find grace to help in time of need.

Hebrews 4:16 (NASB)

Be strong and courageous, do not be afraid or tremble at them,
for the Lord your God is the one who goes with you.
He will not fail you or forsake you.

Deuteronomy 31:6 (NASB)

Cultivating Confidence as ENTREPRENEURS

Under this banner, we'll talk about growing in godly confidence in business and ministry, to build a connected community; to hear and believe and respond to obey God in business and ministry; identity and enemies of your identity in Christ; influence and impact; messaging, branding and building; working God's way fundamentals; our assignment and unique calling; alignment with His precepts; kingdom marketing, sales, sales conversations, closing the sale, pricing with purpose, client engagement, confrontation, generosity, and collaboration without competition; unlearning things that don't align with working God's way; cooperating with the greatness of God; saying yes, saying no; and more. What else can you think of that will help you grow in confidence and serve the Lord?

Whatever you do, do your work heartily, as for the Lord
rather than for men, knowing that from the Lord
you will receive the reward of the inheritance.
It is the Lord Christ whom you serve.

Colossians 3:23-24 (NASB)

The Jeremiah Children Series

How many times in your growing years have you thought to yourself or exclaimed out loud, "If I'd only known?"

We'd love to work and write together to teach our children and 'grandorables' to glean confidence from the Lord in their younger years! Then they can say, "I'm so grateful that I knew that or the Lord taught me that at such a young age!"

The Young Adult Series

As we wrote this first book, we had a young teen offer to tell her story of challenging transitions and how God brought her through some very difficult times. We hoped to include her story in the book right after her mother's story so our readers could see God's hand in family crises and healing from multiple viewpoints. Perhaps we can persuade her to write with us in the next book.

We've begun to dream of a book in the series on cultivating confidence from the Lord in those teen and young adult years written by their peers. Wouldn't that be exciting!

Would you like to join us? If you are interested in helping us write and edit and compile future books in the Cultivating Confidence from the Lord Series, please contact Karen at karen@rhem3eservices.com.

If you are interested in writing your own book or anthology with others, we'd love to share how we do it and help you along the way. We, at RHEMA, are a Shepherd or Hybrid Publishing House offering you an opportunity to co-design your own book contract based on your individual needs. Please contact Lee Desmond at manager@rhemapublishinghouse.com.

About Dr. Karen Lindwall-Bourg, Anthology Compiler, Author

Karen is the Founder of RHEMA 3E Services with her husband Fred. She inspires confidence in others—by cultivating **F**aith, **E**nlightening, **E**ncouraging, and **E**quipping—as they **S**eek the Lord through her call to counseling, coaching, and writing & publishing (F.E.E.E.S.). She has been working with families in crisis since 1995, with Christian entrepreneurs since 2009, and in writing and publishing since 2011. https://amazon.com/author/karenlindwall-bourg

Karen's first publication was commissioned by a publishing company for grief and loss materials. She has often described writing that book as a painstaking process and remarked she is surprised she ever wrote again. She joined a few very powerful writing groups online and attended a writing retreat that changed her trepidation to passion—for reading, writing, and helping others to write and publish—with the founding of RHEMA Publishing House (RPH) in 2012. Through RPH she now leads Retreat to Write © Experiences all across the United States several times a year to help writers get those inspired and life-changing words on paper and into print.

Karen and Fred's lives pretty much revolve around serving the Lord and their family. They have six children and 14 *grandorables* (eight girls, six boys). They are transitioning from a farm—sometimes fondly called a ranchette—in Melissa, Texas, to a smaller farm in Farmersville (cute, huh!), Texas, hoping to enjoy the comforts of both farm living and close proximity to a thriving city in one of the fastest growing counties in the country. She loves writing, reading, fall colors, sunsets over the lake, Great Pyrenees (our "Gentle Giants"), and all her peeps! https://rhema3eservices.com

About Danika Deva, Anthology Editor, Author

With upbeat, joyous enthusiasm, Danika Deva, author, speaker, and content curator inspires others with practical solutions for everyday life and business. Danika is a wife, mother, educator, and hope dealer. She is the director of Operation Freedom Sweep which specializes in helping others "get unstuck" from the baggage in their lives. She also trains churches in the process to use with their congregations.

Her speaking and media appearances include Joni and Friends, NACWE Conferences and Webinars, and churches around the country and internationally. Danika is a Jesus-loving, intentionally-living, principality-fighting woman of God who delights in coaching others in the areas of business, hope, and life. She offers simple, life-changing solutions through her writing, speaking, and coaching. bit.ly/DanikaDevaonAmazon

Her God-given Ph.D. in Hard Knocks and God Rocks has equipped her to inspire others to Be Intentional and to choose joy and hope in hardship so they can not only heal, but flourish.

https://DanikaDeva.com

about the National Association of Christian Women Entrepreneurs

Book 1 of Cultivating Confidence from the Lord: in Life, through Trials, and as Entrepreneurs is written by members of the National Association of Christian Women Entrepreneurs. https://nacwe.com

NACWE is a connected community of like-minded, women entrepreneurs, founded to facilitate a space for networking, education, and support for business owners who love Jesus and are seeking to grow in alignment with their faith, all with a missional focus—who desire to serve the Lord in life and work. They chose Proverbs 3:26 as their key verse for the year 2022: *For the Lord will be your confidence and will keep your foot from being caught (NASB).* And the blessings that have poured from these words are too numerous to count. Let's continue to seek confidence from the Lord together.

We are accomplished Kingdom writing coaches. Under the RPH umbrella, we host and lead several virtual and in-person writing retreats each year to help you write copy for your business and write other works the Lord leads you to. Join us! https://rhema3eservices. com/retreattowrite

We are a team of excellent proofreaders, editors, layout, and design personnel. We're interested in helping you get your book to market and have a variety of services to offer you for both your writing and publishing needs.

Our Mission:

- to help you hit the floor running or writing;
- to take the intimidation out of and add inspiration into publishing your words;
- to help you design a plan for your book that fits your unique needs;
- to seek excellence and adhere to Christian core values.

I love, love, love the written word and the feeling you get when you just have to put your ideas on paper or you'll burst! It thrills me to open a newly published project – it's like Christmas each time.

~Karen Lindwall-Bourg, Founder https://rhemapublishinghouse.com

When Karen approached me about working with RPH, I didn't have to think long before I gave her an answer. Words are so important—I believe they can feed souls or break hearts—and either way, our lives get caught somewhere in the middle of the stories they create.

~Lee Desmond, Managing Director/Editor